MEN-OF-WAR
1770 –1970

J. M. THORNTON

Model and Allied Publications
Argus Books, 14 St James Road,
Watford, Hertfordshire

First published 1978

© J. M. Thornton, 1978
© Argus Books Ltd., 1978

ISBN 0 85242 610 0

Printed and bound in Great Britain by
A. Wheaton & Co. Ltd., Exeter

CONTENTS

PREFACE   5

Part One   AGE OF TRANSITION   7

The Age of Transition (8)   Freaks of the French Fleet (9)   The Last Pre-Dreadnoughts (10)   Warships that Triggered Wars (11)   Torpedo-Boat Carriers (12)   Torpedo-Gunboats and Torpedo-Cruisers (13)   Scouts (14) 'Stringbags' (15)   First Flat Tops (16)   Design Details of Pre-War Aircraft Carriers (17)   Naval Paddle-Wheelers (18)   The Last Battlecruisers (19) The Largest Guns Afloat (20)   'Second Hand' Armaments (21)

Part Two   MEMORIALS AND MEMORIES   22

Hallmarks of History (23)   The Last of the 'Wooden Walls' (24)   From Battle Line to 'Backwater' (25)   Relics of the Past (26)   Memorials of a Bygone Era (27)   U.S. Battleship Memorials (28)   Naval Relics (29)   Destroyer Museums (30)   Memorial Monster and Midgets (31)   U.S. Submarine Memorials (32)   Submarines Preserved (33)   Submarine Relics (34) 'Fragments of the Fleet' (35)   Historic Naval Guns (36)   Naval Remnants (37)   Dry-Land Warships (38)   Naval Mock-ups (39)

Part Three   WARSHIPS THAT MIGHT HAVE BEEN   40

Ships That Never Sailed (41)   Naval Dreams (42)   Cancelled Giants (43) Cancelled Cruisers (44)   Soviet Aspirations (45)

Part Four   SMALL BATTLE UNITS   46

Small Battle Units (47)   Naval 'Hornets' of World War Two (48)   Modern Midgets (49)   Midget Submersibles (50)   Mini-Subs of World War Two (51)   Underwater Midgets (52)   Mini-Cruisers (53)

Part Five   FOR THOSE IN PERIL   54

The Perils of the Sea (55)   'Disasters' Executed (56)   Standing into
Danger (57)   Costly Collisons (58)   Naval Disasters (59)   Carrier
Collisions (60)   The Perils of Submarining (61)   Friendly Enemies (62)
Cataclysmic Catastrophes (63)   Ships that 'Committed Suicide' (64)

Part Six   SECOND CAREERS FOR WARSHIPS   65

Warships Converted into Merchantmen (66)   Ex-Aircraft Carriers (67)
Ex-Warships (68)   Ex-Warriors (69)   Second Lives for Warships (70)
From Sword to Ploughshare (71)   Double Lives (72)   'Civilianized
Invaders' (73)   Royal Yachts (74)   Imperial Yachts (75)   Yachts at
War (76)   Yachts in Grey (77)   The 'Bangor' Sweepers (78)   Training
Ships (79)

Part Seven   NAVAL VIGNETTES   80

Modern Mutinies (81)   Naval Rebellions (82)   Naval Insurgencies (83)
Naval Insurrections (84)   'Davids and Goliaths' (85)   Astonishing
Actions (86)   Target Ships (87)   Retired Battleships (88)   Second
Careers (89)   Famous Flotillas (90)   Warships that 'Changed Sides' (91)
Warships that Changed Flags (92)   Naval Switches (93)   Multi-Lived
Submarines (94)   Captured Submarines (95)   Early Submarine Aircraft
Carriers (96)   Early Landing Ships (97)   The 'Battles' (98)

GLOSSARY   99

INDEX OF SHIPS   102

PREFACE

THERE HAS recently been a resurgence of public interest in military and naval history, particularly pertaining to the events of the twentieth century. A veritable spate of books has subsequently appeared on the market detailing specific and general accounts of battles, campaigns and military hardware. This book does not intend to elaborate on an already well-covered field, but rather to touch on many of the incidental and lesser-known facts and occurrences which sprinkle and add colour, if not substance, to the major events of recent naval history.

Using pen-and-ink sketches with brief captions to illustrate these vignettes, I have attempted to provide a selected collection of naval anecdotes, some of which fall into the category of 'trivia' and others bordering the 'believe-it-or-not'. Divided into seven general sections, it is hoped that the subject material will be of interest to the casual naval 'buff' and that it may even stir the imagination of some readers so that they will dig further into the specific incidents and ships referred to in the abbreviated text.

The genesis of this collection was a monthly feature by the author entitled 'Naval Lore Corner' which originally appeared in the Royal Canadian Navy's now defunct monthly magazine *Crowsnest* from 1952 to 1965. Many of those drawings were compended into a previous book *Warships 1860–1970* (published 1973), and this second volume, though complete in itself, contains entirely new and additional drawings and much hitherto unpublished material.

J. M. Thornton
Captain (N), OMM, CD

PART ONE

THE AGE OF TRANSITION

FOR CENTURIES warship design advanced at a snail's pace. A sailor in Drake's *Revenge* would have felt at home in Nelson's *Victory*. Then suddenly, with the dawn of the age of technology and the catalyst of two world wars, the progress in naval design accelerated at a dazzling rate. Steam replaced sail and iron and steel replaced wood. Multi-gunned broadside batteries were replaced by immeasurably more powerful breech-loading guns in turrets that could train on almost any bearing. Ball-shot gave way to devastatingly powerful explosive shells and warships became capable of engaging each other over miles of ocean. But the transition was far from being well defined. Before the road ahead became clear, many experiments and costly mistakes were made. Indeed, some of the new warship types lasted for only a single generation before they were superseded by more advanced ideas.

The major fleets of the world became heterogeneous collections of experimental units, and several decades passed before the new types became standardized and future concepts became clear. The reign of the great armoured ships, however, was to be a short one. By the middle of the twentieth century they had all but disappeared.

THE AGE OF TRANSITION

III-GUN RUSSIAN STEAM/SAIL BATTLESHIP 'IMPERATOR NICOLAI I' (1857) TYPIFIED THE FIRST STEAM BATTLESHIPS. THEY WERE, IN FACT, WOODEN WALLS WITH AUXILIARY STEAM POWER AND THE BROADSIDE BATTERIES REMAINED. HER TOP SPEED WAS 6 KNOTS...

H.M.SHIPS 'DEVASTATION' (1871) AND 'THUNDERER' (1872) WERE THE FIRST MASTLESS TURRET SHIPS IN THE BRITISH BATTLE FLEET. ORIGINALLY ARMED WITH FOUR MUZZLE-LOADING, RIFLED 12-INCH GUNS THEY WERE LATER EQUIPPED WITH 10-INCH BREECH LOADERS...

H.M.S. 'ALEXANDRA' (1875), SHOWN ABOVE AS MODERNIZED IN 1891, WAS A CENTRAL-BATTERY ARMOURED SHIP. THE MULTI-GUNNED BROADSIDE BATTERY OF AN EARLIER AGE HAD GIVEN WAY TO A FEW VERY LARGE GUNS GROUPED IN A CENTRAL BATTERY. THEIR ARCS OF FIRE, HOWEVER, WERE STILL GREATLY RESTRICTED...

THE VICKERS-BUILT CHINESE CRUISER 'LUNG WEI' (1881) WAS AN EXAMPLE OF A SHIP EQUIPPED WITH FIXED TURRETS. HER HUGE 35-TON 11-INCH GUNS COULD BE TRAINED TO A SMALL DEGREE ON TURNTABLES WITHIN THE FIXED TURRETS..

H.M.S. 'EDINBURGH' AND HER SISTER H.M.S. 'COLOSSUS' (1882) WERE THE FIRST BRITISH CAPITAL SHIPS TO MOUNT BREECH-LOADERS. THEIR TWO REVOLVABLE TURRETS WERE SET 'EN ECHELON' AMIDSHIPS AND EACH CONTAINED TWO 12-INCH GUNS. END-ON FIRE CONTINUED TO BE SEVERELY LIMITED...

FREAKS OF THE FRENCH FLEET
FRANCE SHOWED WORLD LEADERSHIP IN 1859 WITH THE FIRST SEAGOING IRON-CLAD... THE 'GLOIRE'. THEREAFTER HER DESIGNS SEEMED TO HAVE LOST DIRECTION, AND THE FRENCH FLEET BECAME A COLLECTION OF UNHOMO-GENOUS VESSELS, ALMOST NO TWO OF WHICH WERE ALIKE...

MAJOR FRENCH SHIPS OF THIS PERIOD APPEARED CUMBERSOME VESSELS WITH MASSIVE SUPERSTRUCTURES AND MASTS, EXAGGERATED RAM-BOWS, PRONOUNCED TUMBLEHOME AND EITHER GREAT OR LITTLE FREEBOARD...

THE 'HOCHE'(1886)(ABOVE) WAS NICKNAMED 'THE GRAND HOTEL' BECAUSE OF HER COMPLICATED AND ODD SUPER-STRUCTURE. HER TWO 13.4-INCH GUNS WERE DIS-POSED IN TWO CLOSED TURRETS (FORE AND AFT) AND TWO OPEN BARBETTES CONTAINED SINGLE 9.4 s....

THE ARMOUR-PLATED COAST DEFENCE SHIP 'TONNERRE' (1875)(ABOVE) MOUNTED TWO 10.8-INCH GUNS IN A SINGLE CLOSED TURRET FORWARD. SEA SPEED WAS 6 TO 8 KNOTS...

THE COAST DEFENCE SHIP 'TONNANT'(1880)(ABOVE), CARRIED TWO 13.3-INCH GUNS AND WAS HEAVILY ARMOURED. SPEED 10 KNOTS...

BATTLESHIP 'BRENNUS'(ABOVE)(1891) SUFFERED FROM LOW FREEBOARD FOR-WARD. IN A CLASS BY HERSELF, SHE DISPLACED 11,370 TONS AND MOUNTED A MAIN ARMAMENT OF THREE 13.4-INCH GUNS...

'FORMIDABLE'(1885) AS RECONSTRUCTED IN 1897 WITH THREE 14.5-INCH GUNS IN THREE SINGLE TURRETS. HER SPEED WAS 14.5 KNOTS, AND UNLIKE MANY OF HER CONTEMPORARIES, SHE HAD A NEAR-SISTER, THE 'AMIRAL BAUDIN'...

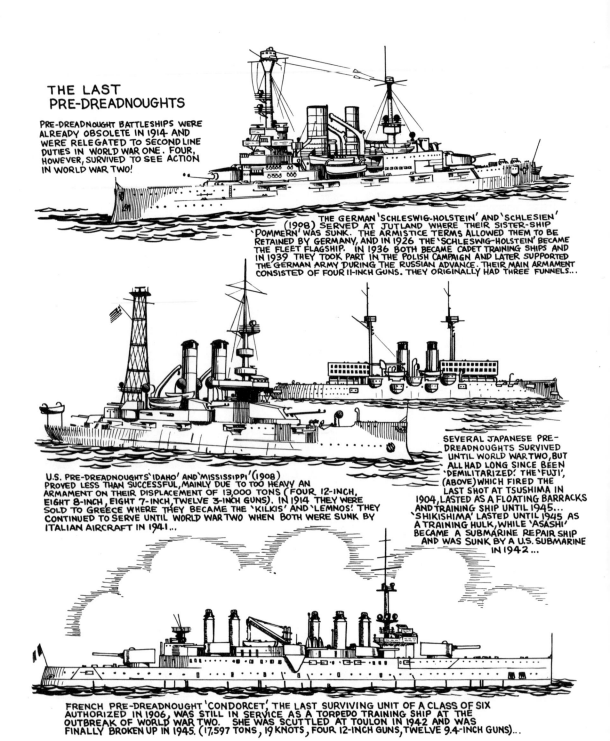

THE LAST PRE-DREADNOUGHTS

PRE-DREADNOUGHT BATTLESHIPS WERE ALREADY OBSOLETE IN 1914 AND WERE RELEGATED TO SECOND LINE DUTIES IN WORLD WAR ONE. FOUR, HOWEVER, SURVIVED TO SEE ACTION IN WORLD WAR TWO!

THE GERMAN 'SCHLESWIG-HOLSTEIN' AND 'SCHLESIEN' (1908) SERVED AT JUTLAND WHERE THEIR SISTER-SHIP 'POMMERN' WAS SUNK. THE ARMISTICE TERMS ALLOWED THEM TO BE RETAINED BY GERMANY, AND IN 1926 THE 'SCHLESWIG-HOLSTEIN' BECAME THE FLEET FLAGSHIP. IN 1936 BOTH BECAME CADET TRAINING SHIPS AND IN 1939 THEY TOOK PART IN THE POLISH CAMPAIGN AND LATER SUPPORTED THE GERMAN ARMY DURING THE RUSSIAN ADVANCE. THEIR MAIN ARMAMENT CONSISTED OF FOUR 11-INCH GUNS. THEY ORIGINALLY HAD THREE FUNNELS...

U.S. PRE-DREADNOUGHTS 'IDAHO' AND 'MISSISSIPPI' (1908) PROVED LESS THAN SUCCESSFUL, MAINLY DUE TO TOO HEAVY AN ARMAMENT ON THEIR DISPLACEMENT OF 13,000 TONS (FOUR 12-INCH, EIGHT 8-INCH, EIGHT 7-INCH, TWELVE 3-INCH GUNS). IN 1914 THEY WERE SOLD TO GREECE WHERE THEY BECAME THE 'KILKIS' AND 'LEMNOS'. THEY CONTINUED TO SERVE UNTIL WORLD WAR TWO WHEN BOTH WERE SUNK BY ITALIAN AIRCRAFT IN 1941...

SEVERAL JAPANESE PRE-DREADNOUGHTS SURVIVED UNTIL WORLD WAR TWO, BUT ALL HAD LONG SINCE BEEN 'DEMILITARIZED'. THE 'FUJI', (ABOVE) WHICH FIRED THE LAST SHOT AT TSUSHIMA IN 1904, LASTED AS A FLOATING BARRACKS AND TRAINING SHIP UNTIL 1945... 'SHIKISHIMA' LASTED UNTIL 1945 AS A TRAINING HULK, WHILE 'ASAHI' BECAME A SUBMARINE REPAIR SHIP AND WAS SUNK BY A U.S. SUBMARINE IN 1942...

FRENCH PRE-DREADNOUGHT 'CONDORCET', THE LAST SURVIVING UNIT OF A CLASS OF SIX AUTHORIZED IN 1906, WAS STILL IN SERVICE AS A TORPEDO TRAINING SHIP AT THE OUTBREAK OF WORLD WAR TWO. SHE WAS SCUTTLED AT TOULON IN 1942 AND WAS FINALLY BROKEN UP IN 1945. (17,597 TONS, 19 KNOTS, FOUR 12-INCH GUNS, TWELVE 9.4-INCH GUNS)...

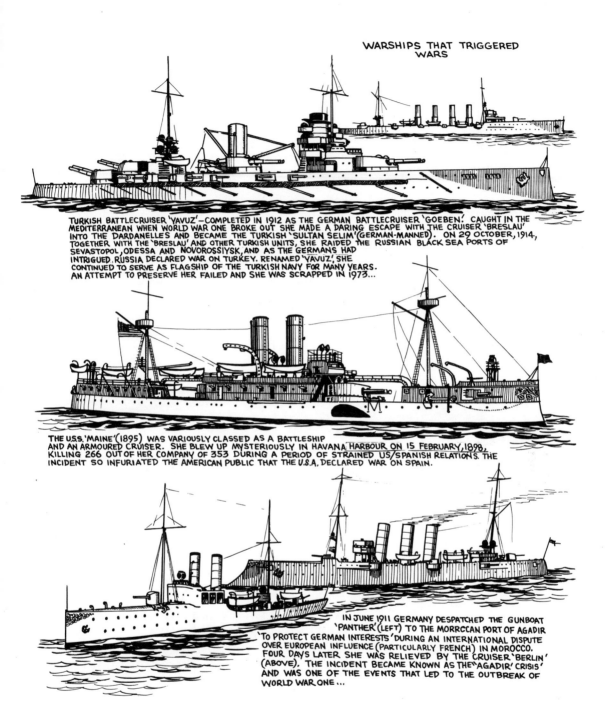

TURKISH BATTLECRUISER 'YAVUZ' – COMPLETED IN 1912 AS THE GERMAN BATTLECRUISER 'GOEBEN'. CAUGHT IN THE MEDITERRANEAN WHEN WORLD WAR ONE BROKE OUT SHE MADE A DARING ESCAPE WITH THE CRUISER 'BRESLAU' INTO THE DARDANELLES AND BECAME THE TURKISH 'SULTAN SELIM' (GERMAN-MANNED). ON 29 OCTOBER, 1914, TOGETHER WITH THE 'BRESLAU' AND OTHER TURKISH UNITS, SHE RAIDED THE RUSSIAN BLACK SEA PORTS OF SEVASTOPOL, ODESSA AND NOVOROSSIYSK, AND AS THE GERMANS HAD INTRIGUED, RUSSIA DECLARED WAR ON TURKEY. RENAMED 'YAVUZ', SHE CONTINUED TO SERVE AS FLAGSHIP OF THE TURKISH NAVY FOR MANY YEARS. AN ATTEMPT TO PRESERVE HER FAILED AND SHE WAS SCRAPPED IN 1973...

THE U.S.S. 'MAINE' (1895) WAS VARIOUSLY CLASSED AS A BATTLESHIP AND AN ARMOURED CRUISER. SHE BLEW UP MYSTERIOUSLY IN HAVANA HARBOUR ON 15 FEBRUARY, 1898, KILLING 266 OUT OF HER COMPANY OF 353 DURING A PERIOD OF STRAINED US/SPANISH RELATIONS. THE INCIDENT SO INFURIATED THE AMERICAN PUBLIC THAT THE U.S.A. DECLARED WAR ON SPAIN.

IN JUNE 1911 GERMANY DESPATCHED THE GUNBOAT 'PANTHER' (LEFT) TO THE MORRCCAN PORT OF AGADIR 'TO PROTECT GERMAN INTERESTS' DURING AN INTERNATIONAL DISPUTE OVER EUROPEAN INFLUENCE (PARTICULARLY FRENCH) IN MOROCCO. FOUR DAYS LATER SHE WAS RELIEVED BY THE CRUISER 'BERLIN' (ABOVE). THE INCIDENT BECAME KNOWN AS THE 'AGADIR' CRISIS' AND WAS ONE OF THE EVENTS THAT LED TO THE OUTBREAK OF WORLD WAR ONE...

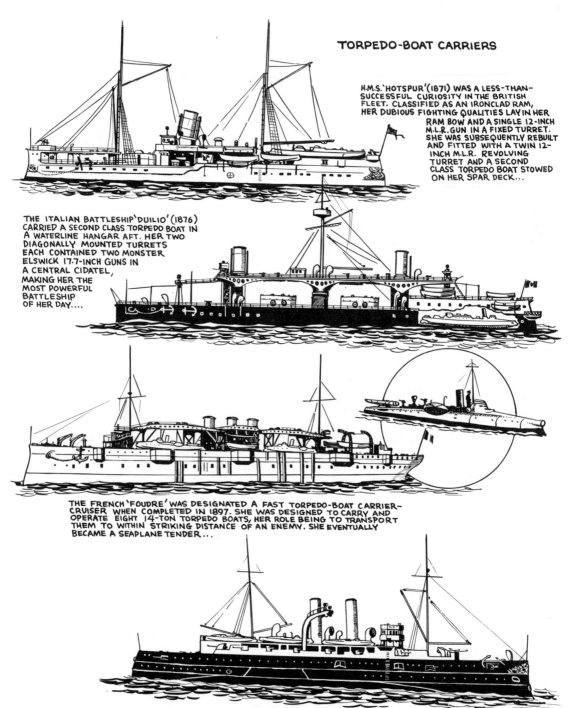

TORPEDO-BOAT CARRIERS

H.M.S. 'HOTSPUR' (1871) WAS A LESS-THAN-SUCCESSFUL CURIOSITY IN THE BRITISH FLEET. CLASSIFIED AS AN IRONCLAD RAM, HER DUBIOUS FIGHTING QUALITIES LAY IN HER RAM BOW AND A SINGLE 12-INCH M.L.R. GUN IN A FIXED TURRET. SHE WAS SUBSEQUENTLY REBUILT AND FITTED WITH A TWIN 12-INCH M.L.R. REVOLVING TURRET AND A SECOND CLASS TORPEDO BOAT STOWED ON HER SPAR DECK...

THE ITALIAN BATTLESHIP 'DUILIO' (1876) CARRIED A SECOND CLASS TORPEDO BOAT IN A WATERLINE HANGAR AFT. HER TWO DIAGONALLY MOUNTED TURRETS EACH CONTAINED TWO MONSTER ELSWICK 17.7-INCH GUNS IN A CENTRAL CIDATEL, MAKING HER THE MOST POWERFUL BATTLESHIP OF HER DAY....

THE FRENCH 'FOUDRE' WAS DESIGNATED A FAST TORPEDO-BOAT CARRIER-CRUISER WHEN COMPLETED IN 1897. SHE WAS DESIGNED TO CARRY AND OPERATE EIGHT 14-TON TORPEDO BOATS, HER ROLE BEING TO TRANSPORT THEM TO WITHIN STRIKING DISTANCE OF AN ENEMY. SHE EVENTUALLY BECAME A SEAPLANE TENDER...

THE BRITISH CRUISER H.M.S. 'VULCAN' (1889) WAS EQUIPPED TO ACCOMMODATE SIX THIRD-CLASS TORPEDO-BOATS. LIKE THE FRENCH 'FOUDRE', SHE WAS IN A CLASS BY HERSELF, AND THE EXPERIMENT WAS NOT REPEATED. SHE REMAINED AFLOAT UNTIL THE 1950's AS PART OF THE COMPOSITE ESTABLISHMENT H.M.S. 'DEFIANCE' AT DEVONPORT...

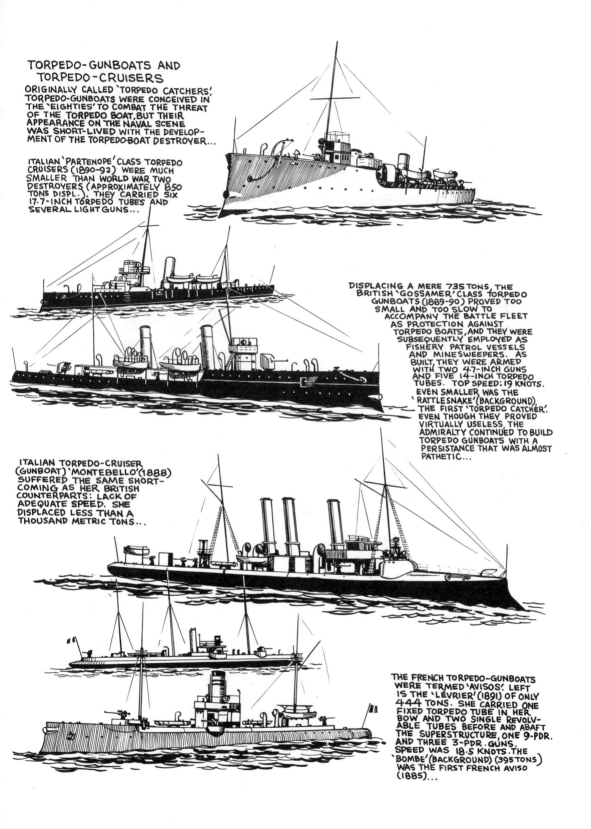

TORPEDO-GUNBOATS AND TORPEDO-CRUISERS

ORIGINALLY CALLED 'TORPEDO CATCHERS', TORPEDO-GUNBOATS WERE CONCEIVED IN THE 'EIGHTIES' TO COMBAT THE THREAT OF THE TORPEDO BOAT, BUT THEIR APPEARANCE ON THE NAVAL SCENE WAS SHORT-LIVED WITH THE DEVELOPMENT OF THE TORPEDO-BOAT DESTROYER...

ITALIAN 'PARTENOPE' CLASS TORPEDO CRUISERS (1890-92) WERE MUCH SMALLER THAN WORLD WAR TWO DESTROYERS (APPROXIMATELY 850 TONS DISPL.). THEY CARRIED SIX 17·7-INCH TORPEDO TUBES AND SEVERAL LIGHT GUNS...

DISPLACING A MERE 735 TONS, THE BRITISH 'GOSSAMER' CLASS TORPEDO GUNBOATS (1889-90) PROVED TOO SMALL AND TOO SLOW TO ACCOMPANY THE BATTLE FLEET AS PROTECTION AGAINST TORPEDO BOATS, AND THEY WERE SUBSEQUENTLY EMPLOYED AS FISHERY PATROL VESSELS AND MINESWEEPERS. AS BUILT, THEY WERE ARMED WITH TWO 4·7-INCH GUNS AND FIVE 14-INCH TORPEDO TUBES. TOP SPEED: 19 KNOTS. EVEN SMALLER WAS THE 'RATTLESNAKE'(BACKGROUND), THE FIRST 'TORPEDO CATCHER'. EVEN THOUGH THEY PROVED VIRTUALLY USELESS, THE ADMIRALTY CONTINUED TO BUILD TORPEDO GUNBOATS WITH A PERSISTANCE THAT WAS ALMOST PATHETIC...

ITALIAN TORPEDO-CRUISER (GUNBOAT) 'MONTEBELLO'(1888) SUFFERED THE SAME SHORT-COMING AS HER BRITISH COUNTERPARTS: LACK OF ADEQUATE SPEED. SHE DISPLACED LESS THAN A THOUSAND METRIC TONS...

THE FRENCH TORPEDO-GUNBOATS WERE TERMED 'AVISOS'. LEFT IS THE 'LÉVRIER'(1891) OF ONLY 444 TONS. SHE CARRIED ONE FIXED TORPEDO TUBE IN HER BOW AND TWO SINGLE REVOLVABLE TUBES BEFORE AND ABAFT THE SUPERSTRUCTURE, ONE 9-PDR. AND THREE 3-PDR. GUNS. SPEED WAS 18·5 KNOTS. THE 'BOMBE'(BACKGROUND) (395 TONS) WAS THE FIRST FRENCH AVISO (1885)...

13

SCOUTS

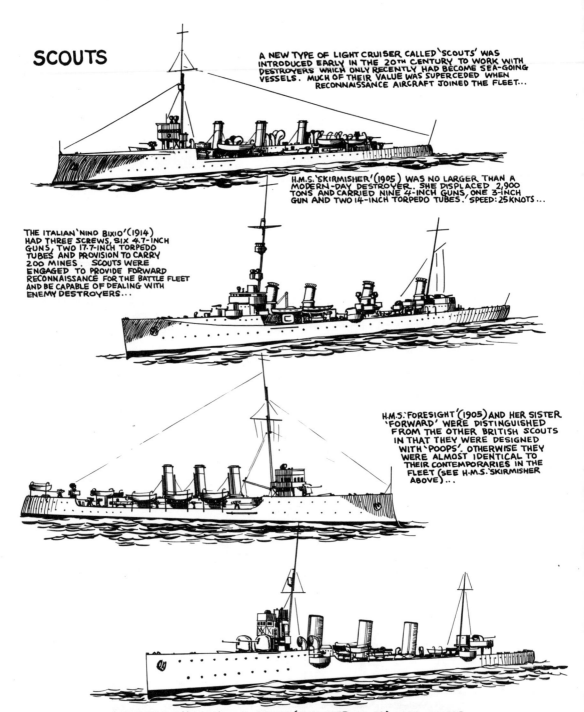

A NEW TYPE OF LIGHT CRUISER CALLED 'SCOUTS' WAS INTRODUCED EARLY IN THE 20TH CENTURY TO WORK WITH DESTROYERS WHICH ONLY RECENTLY HAD BECOME SEA-GOING VESSELS. MUCH OF THEIR VALUE WAS SUPERCEDED WHEN RECONNAISSANCE AIRCRAFT JOINED THE FLEET...

H.M.S. 'SKIRMISHER' (1905) WAS NO LARGER THAN A MODERN-DAY DESTROYER. SHE DISPLACED 2,900 TONS AND CARRIED NINE 4-INCH GUNS, ONE 3-INCH GUN AND TWO 14-INCH TORPEDO TUBES. SPEED: 25 KNOTS...

THE ITALIAN 'NINO BIXIO' (1914) HAD THREE SCREWS, SIX 4.7-INCH GUNS, TWO 17.7-INCH TORPEDO TUBES AND PROVISION TO CARRY 200 MINES. SCOUTS WERE ENGAGED TO PROVIDE FORWARD RECONNAISSANCE FOR THE BATTLE FLEET AND BE CAPABLE OF DEALING WITH ENEMY DESTROYERS...

H.M.S. 'FORESIGHT' (1905) AND HER SISTER 'FORWARD' WERE DISTINGUISHED FROM THE OTHER BRITISH SCOUTS IN THAT THEY WERE DESIGNED WITH 'POOPS'. OTHERWISE THEY WERE ALMOST IDENTICAL TO THEIR CONTEMPORARIES IN THE FLEET (SEE H.M.S. 'SKIRMISHER' ABOVE)...

THE FOUR ITALIAN 'AQUILA' CLASS SCOUTS (COMPLETED 1917-20) WERE ORDERED BY RUMANIA IN 1913 BUT REQUISITIONED BY ITALY IN 1915. FOR SEVERAL YEARS THEY WERE AMONG THE FASTEST WARSHIPS AFLOAT. THE FIRST TWO WERE RECLASSIFIED DESTROYERS IN 1938 AND TRANSFERRED TO NATIONALIST SPAIN. THE SECOND TWO WERE RE-PURCHASED BY RUMANIA AND CONTINUED IN SERVICE AS DESTROYERS UNTIL THE MID-1960s....

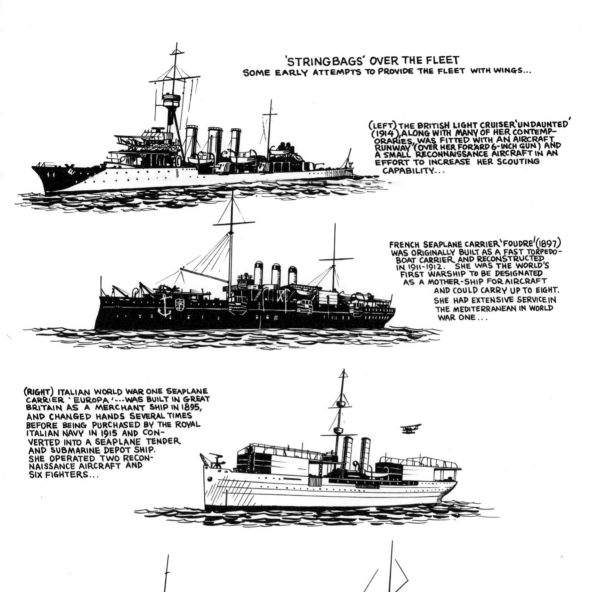

'STRINGBAGS' OVER THE FLEET
SOME EARLY ATTEMPTS TO PROVIDE THE FLEET WITH WINGS...

(LEFT) THE BRITISH LIGHT CRUISER 'UNDAUNTED' (1914), ALONG WITH MANY OF HER CONTEMPORARIES, WAS FITTED WITH AN AIRCRAFT RUNWAY (OVER HER FOR'ARD 6-INCH GUN) AND A SMALL RECONNAISSANCE AIRCRAFT IN AN EFFORT TO INCREASE HER SCOUTING CAPABILITY...

FRENCH SEAPLANE CARRIER 'FOUDRE' (1897) WAS ORIGINALLY BUILT AS A FAST TORPEDO-BOAT CARRIER AND RECONSTRUCTED IN 1911-1912. SHE WAS THE WORLD'S FIRST WARSHIP TO BE DESIGNATED AS A MOTHER-SHIP FOR AIRCRAFT AND COULD CARRY UP TO EIGHT. SHE HAD EXTENSIVE SERVICE IN THE MEDITERRANEAN IN WORLD WAR ONE...

(RIGHT) ITALIAN WORLD WAR ONE SEAPLANE CARRIER 'EUROPA'---WAS BUILT IN GREAT BRITAIN AS A MERCHANT SHIP IN 1895, AND CHANGED HANDS SEVERAL TIMES BEFORE BEING PURCHASED BY THE ROYAL ITALIAN NAVY IN 1915 AND CONVERTED INTO A SEAPLANE TENDER AND SUBMARINE DEPOT SHIP. SHE OPERATED TWO RECONNAISSANCE AIRCRAFT AND SIX FIGHTERS...

RUSSIAN 'HYDRO-CRUISERS' 'IMPERATOR NIKOLAI I' AND 'IMPERATOR ALEXANDER I' WERE BRITISH-BUILT CARGO-LINERS CONVERTED IN 1914 TO HANDLE UP TO EIGHT HYDROPLANES (FLYING BOATS) FOR OPERATIONS AGAINST THE TURKS IN THE BLACK SEA. THEY FORMED THE HYDRO-CRUISER DIVISION OF THE BLACK SEA FLEET, AND SAW MUCH ACTION. THE REDS RENAMED THEM 'AVIATOR' AND 'RESPUBLIKANETZ' IN 1917....

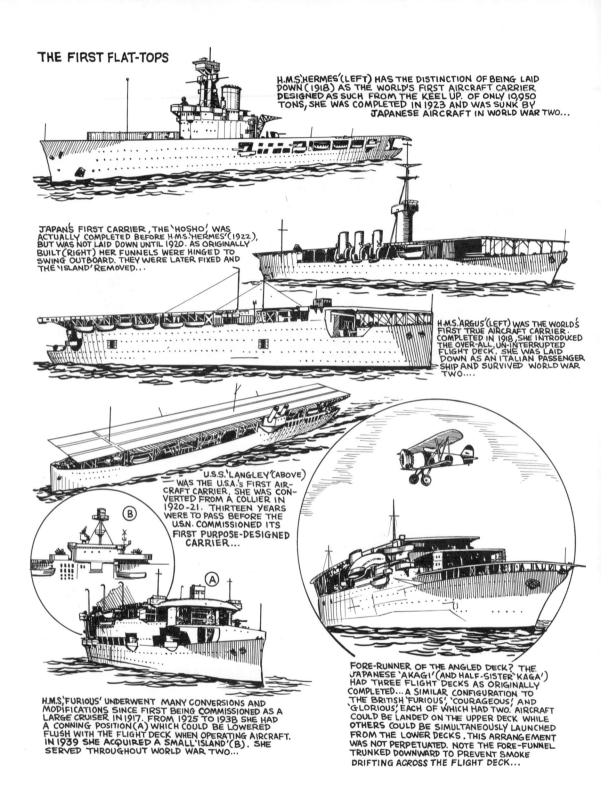

THE FIRST FLAT-TOPS

H.M.S. 'HERMES' (LEFT) HAS THE DISTINCTION OF BEING LAID DOWN (1918) AS THE WORLD'S FIRST AIRCRAFT CARRIER DESIGNED AS SUCH FROM THE KEEL UP. OF ONLY 10,950 TONS, SHE WAS COMPLETED IN 1923 AND WAS SUNK BY JAPANESE AIRCRAFT IN WORLD WAR TWO...

JAPAN'S FIRST CARRIER, THE 'HOSHO' WAS ACTUALLY COMPLETED BEFORE H.M.S. 'HERMES' (1922), BUT WAS NOT LAID DOWN UNTIL 1920. AS ORIGINALLY BUILT (RIGHT) HER FUNNELS WERE HINGED TO SWING OUTBOARD. THEY WERE LATER FIXED AND THE 'ISLAND' REMOVED...

H.M.S. 'ARGUS' (LEFT) WAS THE WORLD'S FIRST TRUE AIRCRAFT CARRIER. COMPLETED IN 1918, SHE INTRODUCED THE OVER-ALL, UN-INTERRUPTED FLIGHT DECK. SHE WAS LAID DOWN AS AN ITALIAN PASSENGER SHIP AND SURVIVED WORLD WAR TWO....

U.S.S. 'LANGLEY' (ABOVE) WAS THE U.S.A.'s FIRST AIRCRAFT CARRIER. SHE WAS CONVERTED FROM A COLLIER IN 1920-21. THIRTEEN YEARS WERE TO PASS BEFORE THE U.S.N. COMMISSIONED ITS FIRST PURPOSE-DESIGNED CARRIER...

H.M.S. 'FURIOUS' UNDERWENT MANY CONVERSIONS AND MODIFICATIONS SINCE FIRST BEING COMMISSIONED AS A LARGE CRUISER IN 1917. FROM 1925 TO 1938 SHE HAD A CONNING POSITION (A) WHICH COULD BE LOWERED FLUSH WITH THE FLIGHT DECK WHEN OPERATING AIRCRAFT. IN 1939 SHE ACQUIRED A SMALL 'ISLAND' (B). SHE SERVED THROUGHOUT WORLD WAR TWO...

FORE-RUNNER OF THE ANGLED DECK? THE JAPANESE 'AKAGI' (AND HALF-SISTER 'KAGA') HAD THREE FLIGHT DECKS AS ORIGINALLY COMPLETED... A SIMILAR CONFIGURATION TO THE BRITISH 'FURIOUS', 'COURAGEOUS', AND 'GLORIOUS', EACH OF WHICH HAD TWO. AIRCRAFT COULD BE LANDED ON THE UPPER DECK WHILE OTHERS COULD BE SIMULTANEOUSLY LAUNCHED FROM THE LOWER DECKS. THIS ARRANGEMENT WAS NOT PERPETUATED. NOTE THE FORE-FUNNEL TRUNKED DOWNWARD TO PREVENT SMOKE DRIFTING ACROSS THE FLIGHT DECK...

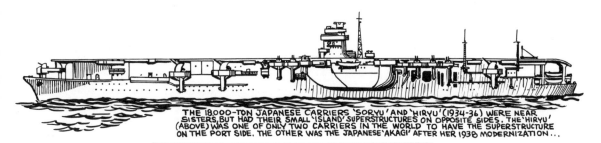

THE 18000-TON JAPANESE CARRIERS 'SORYU' AND 'HIRYU' (1934-36) WERE NEAR SISTERS, BUT HAD THEIR SMALL 'ISLAND' SUPERSTRUCTURES ON OPPOSITE SIDES. THE 'HIRYU' (ABOVE) WAS ONE OF ONLY TWO CARRIERS IN THE WORLD TO HAVE THE SUPERSTRUCTURE ON THE PORT SIDE. THE OTHER WAS THE JAPANESE 'AKAGI' AFTER HER 1938 MODERNIZATION...

DESIGN DETAILS OF PRE-WAR AIRCRAFT CARRIERS

MASSIVE FUNNELS OF U.S.S. 'SARATOGA' AND U.S.S. 'LEXINGTON' (1927-28) KEPT FURNACE FUMES FAR ABOVE THEIR FLIGHT DECKS. LAID DOWN AS BATTLECRUISERS, THEY WERE COMPLETED AS AIRCRAFT CARRIERS...

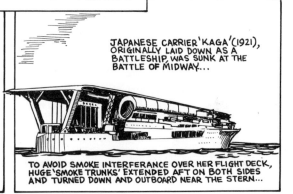

JAPANESE CARRIER 'KAGA' (1921), ORIGINALLY LAID DOWN AS A BATTLESHIP, WAS SUNK AT THE BATTLE OF MIDWAY...

TO AVOID SMOKE INTERFERANCE OVER HER FLIGHT DECK, HUGE 'SMOKE TRUNKS' EXTENDED AFT ON BOTH SIDES AND TURNED DOWN AND OUTBOARD NEAR THE STERN...

THE U.S.S. 'RANGER' (1934) WAS THE U.S.A.'s FIRST CARRIER LAID DOWN AS SUCH. HER SIX FUNNELS COULD BE SWUNG OUT HORIZONTALLY TO AVOID SMOKE FOULING THE DECK...

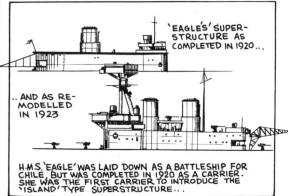

'EAGLE'S' SUPER-STRUCTURE AS COMPLETED IN 1920...

.. AND AS RE-MODELLED IN 1923

H.M.S. 'EAGLE' WAS LAID DOWN AS A BATTLESHIP FOR CHILE, BUT WAS COMPLETED IN 1920 AS A CARRIER. SHE WAS THE FIRST CARRIER TO INTRODUCE THE 'ISLAND' TYPE SUPERSTRUCTURE...

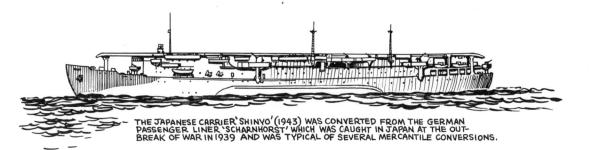

THE JAPANESE CARRIER 'SHINYO' (1943) WAS CONVERTED FROM THE GERMAN PASSENGER LINER 'SCHARNHORST' WHICH WAS CAUGHT IN JAPAN AT THE OUT-BREAK OF WAR IN 1939 AND WAS TYPICAL OF SEVERAL MERCANTILE CONVERSIONS.

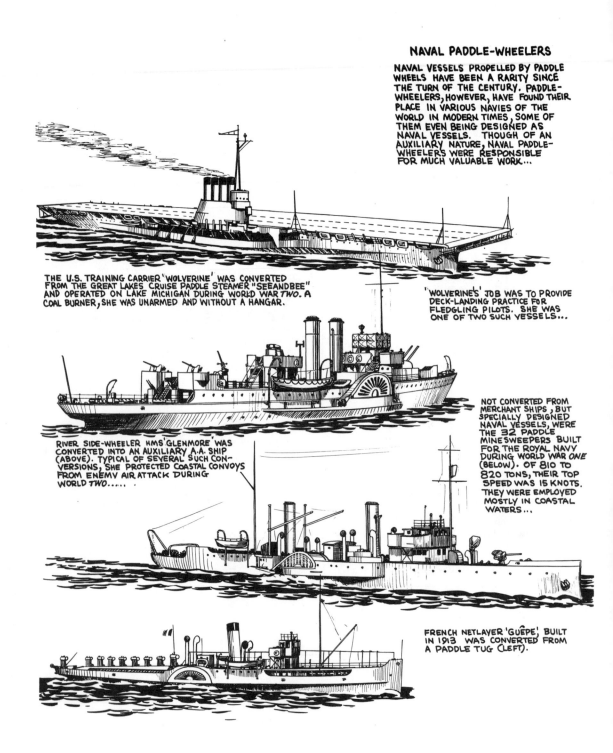

NAVAL PADDLE-WHEELERS

NAVAL VESSELS PROPELLED BY PADDLE WHEELS HAVE BEEN A RARITY SINCE THE TURN OF THE CENTURY. PADDLE-WHEELERS, HOWEVER, HAVE FOUND THEIR PLACE IN VARIOUS NAVIES OF THE WORLD IN MODERN TIMES, SOME OF THEM EVEN BEING DESIGNED AS NAVAL VESSELS. THOUGH OF AN AUXILIARY NATURE, NAVAL PADDLE-WHEELERS WERE RESPONSIBLE FOR MUCH VALUABLE WORK...

THE U.S. TRAINING CARRIER 'WOLVERINE' WAS CONVERTED FROM THE GREAT LAKES CRUISE PADDLE STEAMER "SEEANDBEE" AND OPERATED ON LAKE MICHIGAN DURING WORLD WAR TWO. A COAL BURNER, SHE WAS UNARMED AND WITHOUT A HANGAR.

'WOLVERINE'S' JOB WAS TO PROVIDE DECK-LANDING PRACTICE FOR FLEDGLING PILOTS. SHE WAS ONE OF TWO SUCH VESSELS...

RIVER SIDE-WHEELER HMS 'GLENMORE' WAS CONVERTED INTO AN AUXILIARY A.A. SHIP (ABOVE). TYPICAL OF SEVERAL SUCH CONVERSIONS, SHE PROTECTED COASTAL CONVOYS FROM ENEMY AIR ATTACK DURING WORLD TWO......

NOT CONVERTED FROM MERCHANT SHIPS, BUT SPECIALLY DESIGNED NAVAL VESSELS, WERE THE 32 PADDLE MINESWEEPERS BUILT FOR THE ROYAL NAVY DURING WORLD WAR ONE (BELOW). OF 810 TO 820 TONS, THEIR TOP SPEED WAS 15 KNOTS. THEY WERE EMPLOYED MOSTLY IN COASTAL WATERS...

FRENCH NETLAYER 'GUÊPE', BUILT IN 1913 WAS CONVERTED FROM A PADDLE TUG (LEFT).

THE LAST BATTLECRUISERS

THE BATTLECRUISER CONCEPT OF A FAST CAPITAL SHIP CONCEIVED EARLY IN THE 20TH CENTURY ON THE PRINCIPLE THAT 'SPEED WAS ARMOUR', WAS SHORT-LIVED. IT WAS SOON OUTMODED BY THE FAST BATTLESHIP AND ONLY A FEW VESSELS WITH BATTLECRUISER CHARACTERISTICS WERE BUILT AFTER WORLD WAR ONE...

FRENCH 'DUNKERQUE' AND 'STRASBOURG' (1937-38) WERE BUILT TO COUNTER THE GERMAN 'SCHARNHORST' CLASS. ARMED WITH EIGHT 13-INCH AND SIXTEEN 5.1-INCH GUNS ON A DISPLACEMENT OF 26,500 TONS, THEY COULD MAKE 29.5 KNOTS. BOTH SHIPS WERE SCUTTLED IN THE AUTUMN OF 1942 AT TOULON...

THE 'SCHARNHORST' AND 'GNEISENAU' (1936) WERE THE ULTIMATE GERMAN BATTLECRUISER DESIGN, COMBINING MAXIMUM PROTECTION, SPEED AND FIRE-POWER. DISPLACING 26,000 TONS, THEY WERE ARMED WITH NINE 11-INCH AND TWELVE 5.9-INCH GUNS (SPEED 32 KNOTS). 'GNEISENAU' WAS TO BE RE-ARMED WITH SIX 15-INCH GUNS, BUT THE WAR'S END PREVENTED THIS...

THE U.S. 'ALASKA' CLASS (1943) OF WHICH ONLY TWO UNITS ('ALASKA' AND 'GUAM') WERE COMPLETED WERE OFFICIALLY RATED AS LARGE CRUISERS, AND INDEED REPRESENTED THE ULTIMATE IN CONVENTIONAL CRUISER DESIGN. DISPLACEMENT WAS 27,500 TONS (32,000 FULL LOAD) AND ARMAMENT INCLUDED NINE 12-INCH AND TWELVE 5-INCH GUNS. TOP SPEED WAS 33 KNOTS...
(BELOW)

THE GIANT 'ALASKA' CLASS WERE THE LARGEST 'CRUISERS' EVER BUILT. THEY OWED THEIR GENESIS TO THE UNFOUNDED RUMOUR THAT JAPAN WAS BUILDING SIMILAR ARMOURED VESSELS. FOUR SISTER SHIPS WERE NEVER COMPLETED...

THE LARGEST GUNS AFLOAT

IN MODERN NAVAL ORDNANCE, THE LARGEST
WEAPONS FOUND GENERALLY PRACTICAL
WERE THOSE OF 16-INCH CALIBRE. HOWEVER,
EVEN LARGER GUNS WERE ATTEMPTED... AND
IN SOME CASES PROVED LESS THAN SATISFACTORY...

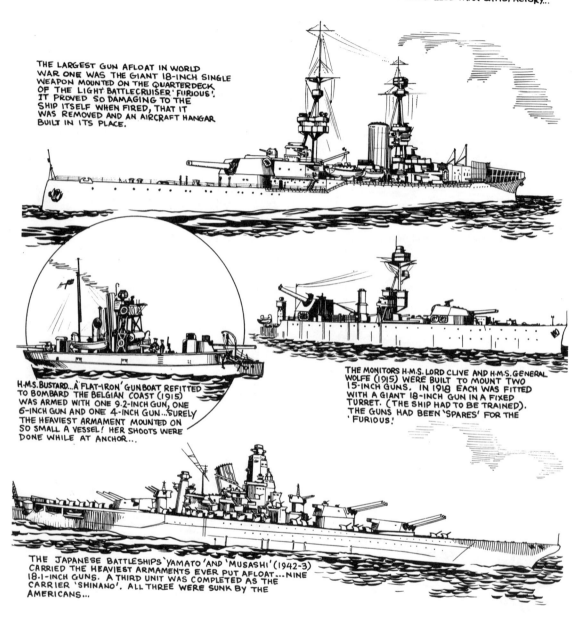

THE LARGEST GUN AFLOAT IN WORLD
WAR ONE WAS THE GIANT 18-INCH SINGLE
WEAPON MOUNTED ON THE QUARTERDECK
OF THE LIGHT BATTLECRUISER 'FURIOUS'.
IT PROVED SO DAMAGING TO THE
SHIP ITSELF WHEN FIRED, THAT IT
WAS REMOVED AND AN AIRCRAFT HANGAR
BUILT IN ITS PLACE.

H·M·S. BUSTARD...A 'FLAT-IRON' GUNBOAT REFITTED
TO BOMBARD THE BELGIAN COAST (1915)
WAS ARMED WITH ONE 9·2-INCH GUN, ONE
6-INCH GUN AND ONE 4-INCH GUN...SURELY
THE HEAVIEST ARMAMENT MOUNTED ON
SO SMALL A VESSEL! HER SHOOTS WERE
DONE WHILE AT ANCHOR...

THE MONITORS H·M·S. LORD CLIVE AND H·M·S. GENERAL
WOLFE (1915) WERE BUILT TO MOUNT TWO
15-INCH GUNS. IN 1918 EACH WAS FITTED
WITH A GIANT 18-INCH GUN IN A FIXED
TURRET. (THE SHIP HAD TO BE TRAINED).
THE GUNS HAD BEEN 'SPARES' FOR THE
'FURIOUS'.

THE JAPANESE BATTLESHIPS 'YAMATO' AND 'MUSASHI' (1942-3)
CARRIED THE HEAVIEST ARMAMENTS EVER PUT AFLOAT...NINE
18·1-INCH GUNS. A THIRD UNIT WAS COMPLETED AS THE
CARRIER 'SHINANO'. ALL THREE WERE SUNK BY THE
AMERICANS...

'SECOND HAND ARMAMENTS'

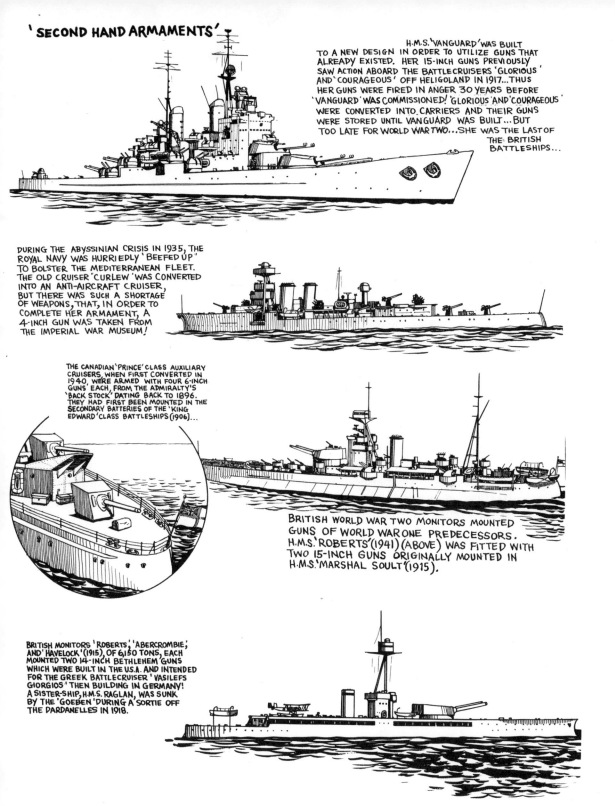

H.M.S. 'VANGUARD' WAS BUILT TO A NEW DESIGN IN ORDER TO UTILIZE GUNS THAT ALREADY EXISTED. HER 15-INCH GUNS PREVIOUSLY SAW ACTION ABOARD THE BATTLECRUISERS 'GLORIOUS' AND 'COURAGEOUS' OFF HELIGOLAND IN 1917... THUS HER GUNS WERE FIRED IN ANGER 30 YEARS BEFORE 'VANGUARD' WAS COMMISSIONED! 'GLORIOUS' AND 'COURAGEOUS' WERE CONVERTED INTO CARRIERS AND THEIR GUNS WERE STORED UNTIL VANGUARD WAS BUILT... BUT TOO LATE FOR WORLD WAR TWO... SHE WAS THE LAST OF THE BRITISH BATTLESHIPS...

DURING THE ABYSSINIAN CRISIS IN 1935, THE ROYAL NAVY WAS HURRIEDLY 'BEEFED UP' TO BOLSTER THE MEDITERRANEAN FLEET. THE OLD CRUISER 'CURLEW' WAS CONVERTED INTO AN ANTI-AIRCRAFT CRUISER, BUT THERE WAS SUCH A SHORTAGE OF WEAPONS, THAT, IN ORDER TO COMPLETE HER ARMAMENT, A 4-INCH GUN WAS TAKEN FROM THE IMPERIAL WAR MUSEUM!

THE CANADIAN 'PRINCE' CLASS AUXILIARY CRUISERS, WHEN FIRST CONVERTED IN 1940, WERE ARMED WITH FOUR 6-INCH GUNS EACH, FROM THE ADMIRALTY'S 'BACK STOCK' DATING BACK TO 1896. THEY HAD FIRST BEEN MOUNTED IN THE SECONDARY BATTERIES OF THE 'KING EDWARD' CLASS BATTLESHIPS (1906)...

BRITISH WORLD WAR TWO MONITORS MOUNTED GUNS OF WORLD WAR ONE PREDECESSORS. H.M.S. 'ROBERTS' (1941) (ABOVE) WAS FITTED WITH TWO 15-INCH GUNS ORIGINALLY MOUNTED IN H.M.S. 'MARSHAL SOULT' (1915).

BRITISH MONITORS 'ROBERTS,' 'ABERCROMBIE,' AND 'HAVELOCK' (1915), OF 6,150 TONS, EACH MOUNTED TWO 14-INCH BETHLEHEM GUNS WHICH WERE BUILT IN THE U.S.A. AND INTENDED FOR THE GREEK BATTLECRUISER 'VASILEFS GIORGIOS' THEN BUILDING IN GERMANY! A SISTER-SHIP, H.M.S. RAGLAN, WAS SUNK BY THE 'GOEBEN' DURING A SORTIE OFF THE DARDANELLES IN 1918.

PART TWO

MEMORIALS
AND MEMORIES

AS THE GREAT battle fleets of the past fade into history and the last of the wartime ships vanish from the seas to be replaced by sleek new vessels armed with guided missiles and festooned with electronic arrays and computerized systems, it is indeed fortunate that interested groups and governments throughout the world have seen fit to preserve relics of the past, which remind us of those bygone days and of the great events in which they figured.

It is still possible to walk the decks of wooden walls and pre-dreadnoughts, some of which have made history in their own right, and to see how the sailors lived and fought and to study the construction and technology of the ships themselves. Indeed, many 'old hands' are convinced that the modern warships of today lack much of the character and aesthetic beauty of their predecessors.

By far the largest collection of warships preserved as memorials, from battleships to submarines, can be seen in the bays, inlets and rivers of America. However, in nearly every nation with a maritime background there can be found these tangible memorials of a now-vanished era.

HALLMARKS of HISTORY...

H.M.S. 'VICTORY' (LEFT) LORD NELSON'S FLAG-SHIP AT THE BATTLE OF TRAFALGAR, IS PERHAPS THE MOST FAMOUS SHIP STILL IN EXISTANCE. BUILT AT CHATHAM BETWEEN 1759 AND 1765 AS A 102-GUN FIRST RATE LINE-OF-BATTLESHIP, SHE SERVED ON ACTIVE DUTY FOR 47 YEARS. PERMANENTLY DOCKED IN 1922, SHE HAS BEEN COMPLETELY RESTORED AS A PERMANENT MEMORIAL, AND WEARS THE FLAG OF THE C.-IN-C. PORTSMOUTH, WHERE SHE IS DRYDOCKED.

U.S. FRIGATE 'CONSTELLATION' (BELOW) LAUNCHED IN 1797 AND NOW ON DISPLAY AT BALTIMORE, IS THE OLDEST WARSHIP STILL AFLOAT. DEDICATED AS A NATIONAL SHRINE IN 1961, SHE FOUGHT AGAINST THE BARBARY PIRATES IN THE WAR OF 1812...

U.S.S. 'CONSTITUTION' (ABOVE) 'OLD IRONSIDES' WAS LAUNCHED IN 1797, AND IS THE SECOND OLDEST WARSHIP AFLOAT. A 44-GUN FRIGATE, SHE HAD A SPECTACULAR CAREER AGAINST THE BARBARY PIRATES AND IN THE WAR OF 1812. SHE SERVED FOR 84 YEARS. NOW RE-TIMBERED AND RE-RIGGED, SHE IS ON DISPLAY AS A NATIONAL SHRINE AT BOSTON, MASS....

H.M.S. AGINCOURT, ONE OF BRITAIN'S FIRST IRON-CLAD BATTLESHIPS (RIGHT) COMPLETED IN 1868. SHE AND HER TWO SISTERS WERE UNIQUE FOR THEIR FIVE MASTS. IN 1908 SHE WAS LAID UP AT SHEERNESS AND CONVERTED INTO A COAL HULK (ABOVE), IN WHICH LOWLY STATION SHE SERVED UNTIL 1960...

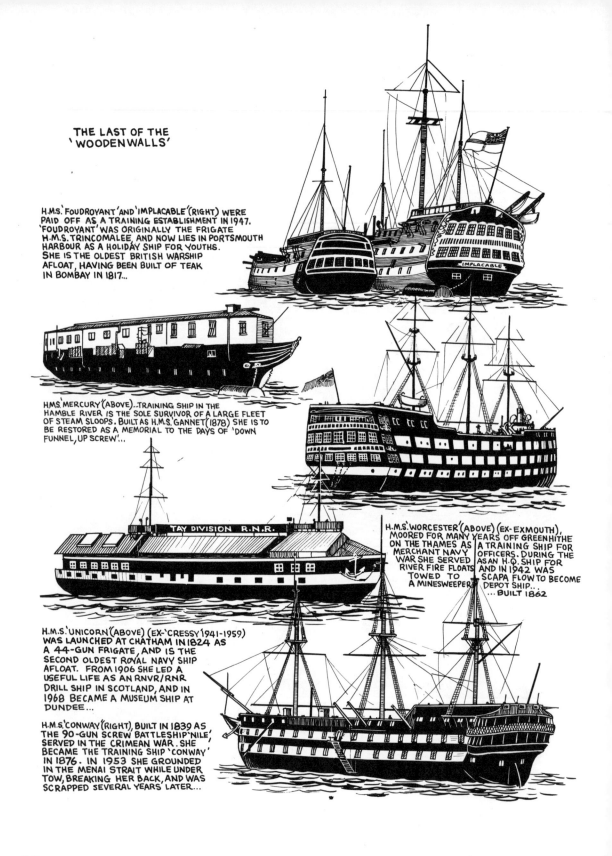

THE LAST OF THE 'WOODEN WALLS'

H.M.S. FOUDROYANT' AND 'IMPLACABLE' (RIGHT) WERE PAID OFF AS A TRAINING ESTABLISHMENT IN 1947. 'FOUDROYANT' WAS ORIGINALLY THE FRIGATE H.M.S. TRINCOMALEE, AND NOW LIES IN PORTSMOUTH HARBOUR AS A HOLIDAY SHIP FOR YOUTHS. SHE IS THE OLDEST BRITISH WARSHIP AFLOAT, HAVING BEEN BUILT OF TEAK IN BOMBAY IN 1817...

H.M.S. MERCURY (ABOVE)...TRAINING SHIP IN THE HAMBLE RIVER IS THE SOLE SURVIVOR OF A LARGE FLEET OF STEAM SLOOPS. BUILT AS H.M.S. GANNET (1878) SHE IS TO BE RESTORED AS A MEMORIAL TO THE DAYS OF 'DOWN FUNNEL, UP SCREW'...

H.M.S. WORCESTER (ABOVE) (EX-EXMOUTH), MOORED FOR MANY YEARS OFF GREENHITHE ON THE THAMES AS A TRAINING SHIP FOR MERCHANT NAVY OFFICERS. DURING THE WAR SHE SERVED AS AN H.Q. SHIP FOR RIVER FIRE FLOATS AND IN 1942 WAS TOWED TO SCAPA FLOW TO BECOME A MINESWEEPER DEPOT SHIP...
...BUILT 1862

H.M.S. UNICORN' (ABOVE) (EX-'CRESSY' 1941-1959) WAS LAUNCHED AT CHATHAM IN 1824 AS A 44-GUN FRIGATE, AND IS THE SECOND OLDEST ROYAL NAVY SHIP AFLOAT. FROM 1906 SHE LED A USEFUL LIFE AS AN RNVR/RNR DRILL SHIP IN SCOTLAND, AND IN 1968 BECAME A MUSEUM SHIP AT DUNDEE...

H.M.S. CONWAY (RIGHT), BUILT IN 1839 AS THE 90-GUN SCREW BATTLESHIP 'NILE' SERVED IN THE CRIMEAN WAR. SHE BECAME THE TRAINING SHIP 'CONWAY' IN 1876. IN 1953 SHE GROUNDED IN THE MENAI STRAIT WHILE UNDER TOW, BREAKING HER BACK, AND WAS SCRAPPED SEVERAL YEARS LATER...

FROM BATTLE LINE TO 'BACKWATER'...

SPANISH PROTECTED CRUISER 'REINA MERCEDES', LAUNCHED IN 1887 AT CARTAGENA WAS CAPTURED BY THE AMERICANS AT SANTIAGO, CUBA AT START OF SPANISH-AMERICAN WAR. THE SPANISH LATER ATTEMPTED TO SINK HER IN THE HARBOUR ENTRANCE TO PREVENT THE AMERICANS ENTERING THE HARBOUR, BUT SHE SANK WITHOUT BLOCKING THE CHANNEL. SALVED AFTER THE WAR BY THE U.S.N. SHE BECAME THE STATION SHIP AT ANNAPOLIS IN 1912 AND FLEW THE ADMIRAL'S FLAG AS H.Q. SHIP FOR THE SEVERN RIVER COMMAND FOR MANY YEARS...

U.S.S. PRAIRIE STATE (BELOW) UNTIL RECENTLY WAS A FLOATING ARMORY FOR A NAVAL RESERVE CENTRE IN NEW YORK. FORMERLY THE BATTLESHIP 'ILLINOIS', A UNIT OF THE 'GREAT WHITE FLEET,' SHE WAS PRESENT AT THE CORONATION NAVAL REVIEW OF KING EDWARD VII AND WAS CONVERTED FOR TRAINING DUTIES IN 1924...

U.S.S. 'INDEPENDENCE' (ABOVE) — AMERICA'S FIRST SHIP-OF-THE-LINE, SERVED FOR NEARLY A CENTURY. LAUNCHED IN 1814 AS A 'SEVENTY-FOUR', SHE EVENTUALLY BECAME THE RECEIVING SHIP AT MARE ISLAND IN SAN FRANCISCO, CONTINUING IN THAT ROLE UNTIL 1912...

ANOTHER SHIP-OF-THE-LINE, 'ALABAMA' (RIGHT) RETIRED AS THE 'NEW HAMPSHIRE' AND FOR MANY YEARS WAS A TRAINING VESSEL FOR NAVAL MILITIA IN NEW YORK...

H.M.S. 'WARRIOR' (1860), THE FIRST IRON-HULLED ARMOURED WARSHIP TO BE LAUNCHED, IS STILL AFLOAT, EMPLOYED AS A COAL HULK AT PEMBROKE DOCK. SHE SERVED AS A DEPOT SHIP IN WORLD WAR TWO, AND IS TO BE RESTORED AS A MUSEUM SHIP AT THE AGE OF OVER 115....

PERUVIAN IRON-CLAD SINGLE TURRET RAM 'HUASCAR'
BUILT IN ENGLAND IN 1865, IS STILL AFLOAT AS A MEMORIAL AT TALCAHUANO, CHILE.
IN 1877, MANNED BY REVOLUTIONARIES WHO HAD MOLESTED BRITISH SHIPS, SHE FOUGHT AN IN-
DECISIVE DAY-LONG BATTLE WITH H.M.SHIPS 'SHAH' AND 'AMETHYST'. DURING THE ACTION SHE
BECAME THE FIRST SHIP AT WHICH A LOCOMOTIVE TORPEDO WAS FIRED. IN 1879 SHE SANK
THE CHILEAN 'ESMERALDA' BUT AT THE BATTLE OF ANGMOS SHE WAS OVER-POWERED BY THE
CHILEAN 'ALMIRANTE COCHRANE' AND 'BLANCO ENCALADA' AND INCORPORATED INTO THE CHILEAN NAVY...

THE DUTCH IRONCLAD RAM 'SCHORPIOEN' BUILT IN FRANCE
IN 1867/8, SERVED FOR 38 YEARS BEFORE BEING 'HULKED'
AS AN ACCOMMODATION SHIP IN 1906. SHE STILL EXISTS
TODAY (LEFT) (AS A FLOATING BARRACKS AT DEN HELDER
FOR WRENS OF THE ROYAL NETHERLANDS NAVY) AS DOES
HER NEAR SISTER 'BUFFEL' WHICH
IS BEING RESTORED AS A MUSEUM...

THE 4,500-TON U.S. CRUISER 'CHICAGO'
(SHOWN RIGHT AFTER MODERNIZATION IN
1899) WAS COMMISSIONED IN 1889
AND SERVED IN THE U.S. FLEET
UNTIL 1923. SHE THEN BECAME A
BARRACK SHIP AT PEARL HARBOR FOR
THE SUBMARINE BASE (BELOW). IN 1928
HER NAME WAS CHANGED TO 'ALTON'...

H.M.A.S. 'CERBERUS'... SMALL 'BREASTWORK' MONITOR COMPLETED
IN 1870 FOR THE DEFENCE OF MELBOURNE HARBOUR
AND NOW BEING RESTORED AS AN HISTORIC RELIC
BY THE MARITIME TRUST OF AUSTRALIA. PAID OFF
IN 1924 AFTER WORLD WAR ONE SERVICE AS A
SUBMARINE DEPOT SHIP, SHE WAS SOLD
AND HAS SERVED AS A BREAKWATER
FOR A YACHT CLUB EVER SINCE.
SHE WAS THE FIRST WARSHIP WITH
A CENTRAL SUPERSTRUCTURE AND
TURRETS FORE AND AFT.
(FOUR 10-INCH GUNS)...

MEMORIALS OF A BYGONE ERA...

ADMIRAL TOGO'S FAMOUS FLAGSHIP IN THE VICTORY OVER RUSSIA IN 1905, THE BATTLESHIP 'MIKASA' BUILT BY VICKERS IN 1902 STILL EXISTS AS A JAPANESE NATIONAL MEMORIAL EMBEDDED IN CONCRETE AT YOKOSUKA. SHE BECAME PART OF AN AMUSEMENT CENTRE IN 1949 BUT WAS RESTORED TO HER ORIGINAL STATE IN 1961... THE ONLY PRE-DREADNOUGHT BATTLESHIP STILL IN EXISTENCE...

U.S.S.'OLYMPIA' MEMORIAL AND MUSEUM. THE OLD PROTECTED CRUISER WHICH BECAME FAMOUS AS ADMIRAL DEWEY'S FLAGSHIP AT THE BATTLE OF KAVITE DURING THE SPANISH-AMERICAN WAR IN 1898 IS PRESERVED AND ON DISPLAY AT PHILADELPHIA. BUILT FROM 1891 TO 1895, SHE IS NOW LOCATED ON THE DELAWARE RIVER...

RUSSIAN CRUISER 'AURORA' (BUILT 1896-1900) AND STILL AFLOAT AS A NATIONAL MEMORIAL. IN 1917, UNDER ORDERS FROM KERENSKY, SHE STEAMED UP THE RIVER NEVA AND SHELLED THE WINTER PALACE IN PETROGRAD. THIS WAS PURPORTED TO BE THE OPENING SHOTS OF THE RUSSIAN REVOLUTION. SHE LIES TODAY AT ANCHOR IN LENINGRAD...

GREEK ARMOURED CRUISER 'AVEROF' (BUILT 1910) GAINED FAME IN THE BALKAN WARS AND CONTINUED AS AN ACTIVE FLEET UNIT THROUGH WORLD WAR TWO. SHE IS NOW PRESERVED AS A NAVAL MUSEUM AT THE GREEK NAVAL ESTABLISHMENT LOCATED AT THE AEGEAN ISLAND OF POROS...

27

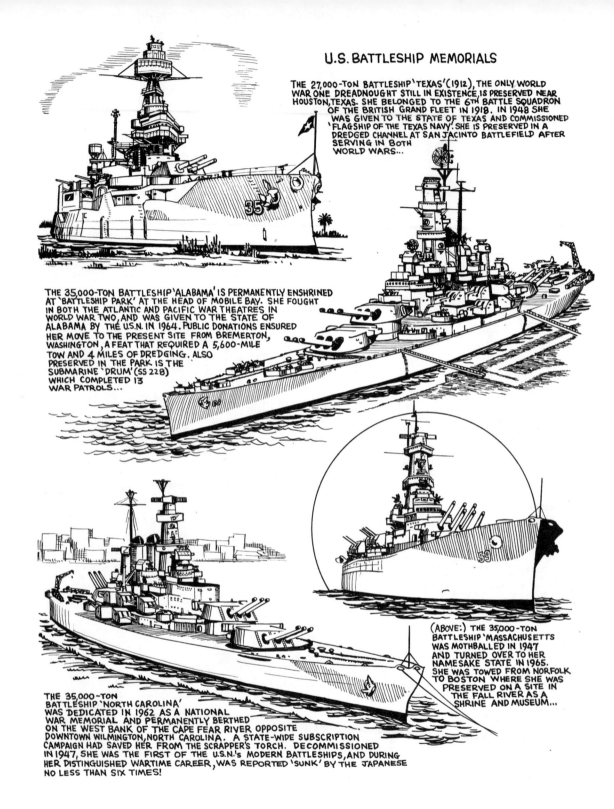

U.S. BATTLESHIP MEMORIALS

THE 27,000-TON BATTLESHIP 'TEXAS' (1912), THE ONLY WORLD WAR ONE DREADNOUGHT STILL IN EXISTENCE, IS PRESERVED NEAR HOUSTON, TEXAS. SHE BELONGED TO THE 6TH BATTLE SQUADRON OF THE BRITISH GRAND FLEET IN 1918. IN 1948 SHE WAS GIVEN TO THE STATE OF TEXAS AND COMMISSIONED 'FLAGSHIP OF THE TEXAS NAVY'. SHE IS PRESERVED IN A DREDGED CHANNEL AT SAN JACINTO BATTLEFIELD AFTER SERVING IN BOTH WORLD WARS...

THE 35,000-TON BATTLESHIP 'ALABAMA' IS PERMANENTLY ENSHRINED AT 'BATTLESHIP PARK' AT THE HEAD OF MOBILE BAY. SHE FOUGHT IN BOTH THE ATLANTIC AND PACIFIC WAR THEATRES IN WORLD WAR TWO, AND WAS GIVEN TO THE STATE OF ALABAMA BY THE U.S.N. IN 1964. PUBLIC DONATIONS ENSURED HER MOVE TO THE PRESENT SITE FROM BREMERTON, WASHINGTON, A FEAT THAT REQUIRED A 5,600-MILE TOW AND 4 MILES OF DREDGING. ALSO PRESERVED IN THE PARK IS THE SUBMARINE 'DRUM' (SS 228) WHICH COMPLETED 13 WAR PATROLS...

(ABOVE:) THE 35,000-TON BATTLESHIP 'MASSACHUSETTS' WAS MOTHBALLED IN 1947 AND TURNED OVER TO HER NAMESAKE STATE IN 1965. SHE WAS TOWED FROM NORFOLK TO BOSTON WHERE SHE WAS PRESERVED ON A SITE IN THE FALL RIVER AS A SHRINE AND MUSEUM...

THE 35,000-TON BATTLESHIP 'NORTH CAROLINA' WAS DEDICATED IN 1962 AS A NATIONAL WAR MEMORIAL AND PERMANENTLY BERTHED ON THE WEST BANK OF THE CAPE FEAR RIVER OPPOSITE DOWNTOWN WILMINGTON, NORTH CAROLINA. A STATE-WIDE SUBSCRIPTION CAMPAIGN HAD SAVED HER FROM THE SCRAPPER'S TORCH. DECOMMISSIONED IN 1947, SHE WAS THE FIRST OF THE U.S.N.'s MODERN BATTLESHIPS, AND DURING HER DISTINGUISHED WARTIME CAREER, WAS REPORTED 'SUNK' BY THE JAPANESE NO LESS THAN SIX TIMES!

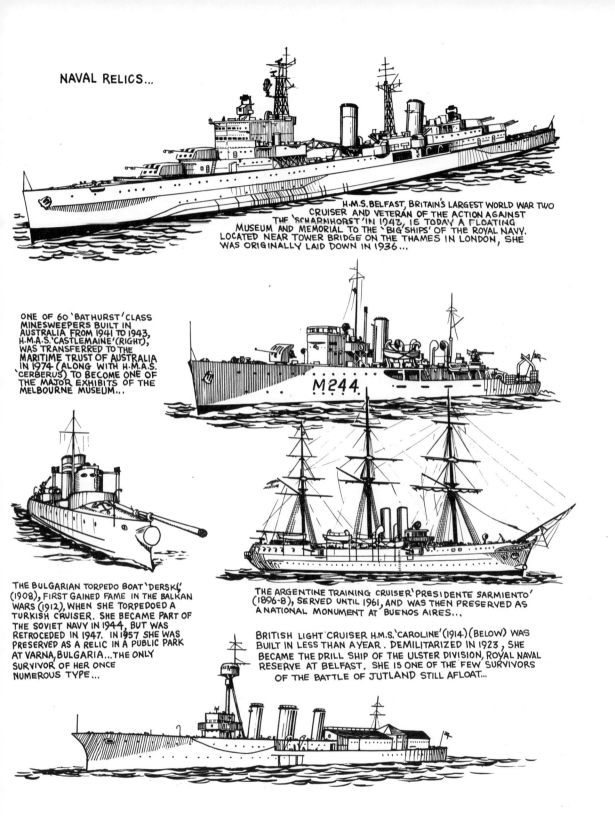

NAVAL RELICS...

H.M.S. BELFAST, BRITAIN'S LARGEST WORLD WAR TWO CRUISER AND VETERAN OF THE ACTION AGAINST THE 'SCHARNHORST' IN 1942, IS TODAY A FLOATING MUSEUM AND MEMORIAL TO THE 'BIG SHIPS' OF THE ROYAL NAVY. LOCATED NEAR TOWER BRIDGE ON THE THAMES IN LONDON, SHE WAS ORIGINALLY LAID DOWN IN 1936...

ONE OF 60 'BATHURST' CLASS MINESWEEPERS BUILT IN AUSTRALIA FROM 1941 TO 1943, H.M.A.S. 'CASTLEMAINE' (RIGHT), WAS TRANSFERRED TO THE MARITIME TRUST OF AUSTRALIA IN 1974 (ALONG WITH H.M.A.S. 'CERBERUS') TO BECOME ONE OF THE MAJOR EXHIBITS OF THE MELBOURNE MUSEUM...

M244

THE BULGARIAN TORPEDO BOAT 'DERSKI' (1908), FIRST GAINED FAME IN THE BALKAN WARS (1912), WHEN SHE TORPEDOED A TURKISH CRUISER. SHE BECAME PART OF THE SOVIET NAVY IN 1944, BUT WAS RETROCEDED IN 1947. IN 1957 SHE WAS PRESERVED AS A RELIC IN A PUBLIC PARK AT VARNA, BULGARIA...THE ONLY SURVIVOR OF HER ONCE NUMEROUS TYPE...

THE ARGENTINE TRAINING CRUISER 'PRESIDENTE SARMIENTO' (1896-8), SERVED UNTIL 1961, AND WAS THEN PRESERVED AS A NATIONAL MONUMENT AT BUENOS AIRES...

BRITISH LIGHT CRUISER H.M.S. 'CAROLINE' (1914) (BELOW) WAS BUILT IN LESS THAN A YEAR. DEMILITARIZED IN 1923, SHE BECAME THE DRILL SHIP OF THE ULSTER DIVISION, ROYAL NAVAL RESERVE AT BELFAST. SHE IS ONE OF THE FEW SURVIVORS OF THE BATTLE OF JUTLAND STILL AFLOAT...

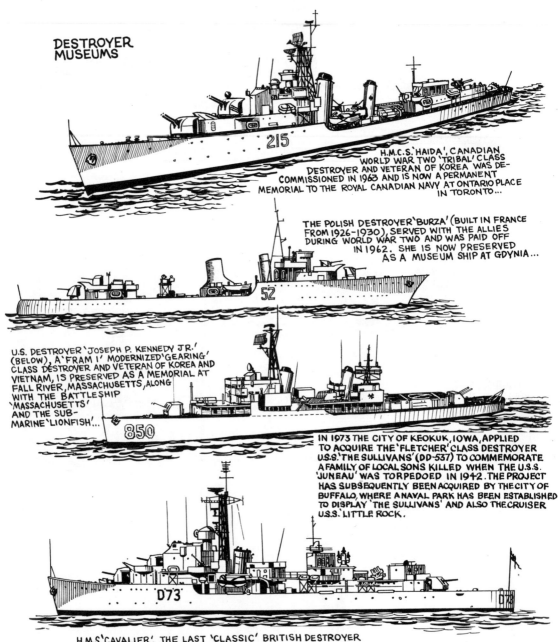

DESTROYER MUSEUMS

H.M.C.S. 'HAIDA', CANADIAN WORLD WAR TWO 'TRIBAL' CLASS DESTROYER AND VETERAN OF KOREA WAS DE-COMMISSIONED IN 1963 AND IS NOW A PERMANENT MEMORIAL TO THE ROYAL CANADIAN NAVY AT ONTARIO PLACE IN TORONTO...

THE POLISH DESTROYER 'BURZA' (BUILT IN FRANCE FROM 1926-1930), SERVED WITH THE ALLIES DURING WORLD WAR TWO AND WAS PAID OFF IN 1962. SHE IS NOW PRESERVED AS A MUSEUM SHIP AT GDYNIA...

U.S. DESTROYER 'JOSEPH P. KENNEDY JR.' (BELOW), A 'FRAM I' MODERNIZED 'GEARING' CLASS DESTROYER AND VETERAN OF KOREA AND VIETNAM, IS PRESERVED AS A MEMORIAL AT FALL RIVER, MASSACHUSETTS, ALONG WITH THE BATTLESHIP 'MASSACHUSETTS' AND THE SUB-MARINE 'LIONFISH'...

IN 1973 THE CITY OF KEOKUK, IOWA, APPLIED TO ACQUIRE THE 'FLETCHER' CLASS DESTROYER U.S.S. 'THE SULLIVANS' (DD-537) TO COMMEMORATE A FAMILY OF LOCAL SONS KILLED WHEN THE U.S.S. 'JUNEAU' WAS TORPEDOED IN 1942. THE PROJECT HAS SUBSEQUENTLY BEEN ACQUIRED BY THE CITY OF BUFFALO, WHERE A NAVAL PARK HAS BEEN ESTABLISHED TO DISPLAY 'THE SULLIVANS' AND ALSO THE CRUISER U.S.S. 'LITTLE ROCK'.

H.M.S. 'CAVALIER', THE LAST 'CLASSIC' BRITISH DESTROYER TO DECOMMISSION (1974) HAS BEEN PRESERVED AS A FLOATING MUSEUM AT SOUTHAMPTON...

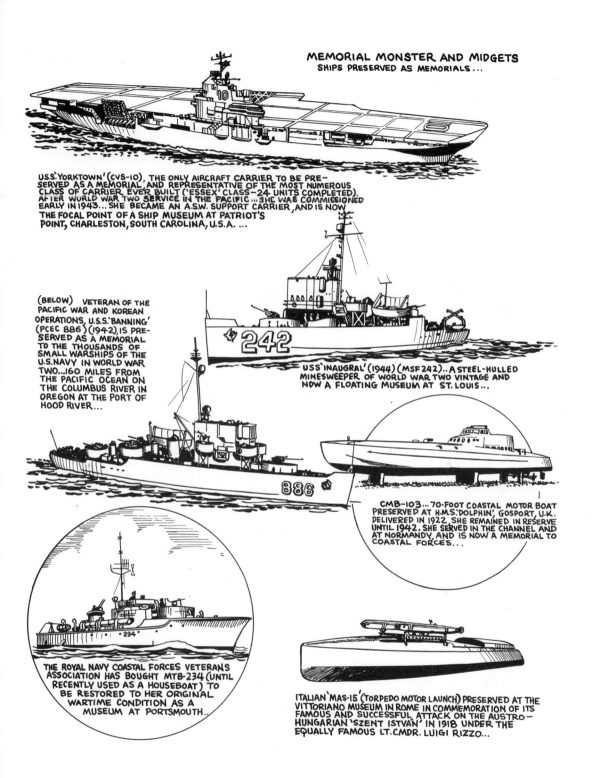

MEMORIAL MONSTER AND MIDGETS
SHIPS PRESERVED AS MEMORIALS...

U.S.S. 'YORKTOWN' (CVS-10), THE ONLY AIRCRAFT CARRIER TO BE PRE-SERVED AS A MEMORIAL, AND REPRESENTATIVE OF THE MOST NUMEROUS CLASS OF CARRIER EVER BUILT ('ESSEX' CLASS—24 UNITS COMPLETED). AFTER WORLD WAR TWO SERVICE IN THE PACIFIC... SHE WAS COMMISSIONED EARLY IN 1943... SHE BECAME AN A.S.W. SUPPORT CARRIER, AND IS NOW THE FOCAL POINT OF A SHIP MUSEUM AT PATRIOT'S POINT, CHARLESTON, SOUTH CAROLINA, U.S.A. ...

(BELOW) VETERAN OF THE PACIFIC WAR AND KOREAN OPERATIONS, U.S.S. 'BANNING' (PCEC 886) (1942), IS PRE-SERVED AS A MEMORIAL TO THE THOUSANDS OF SMALL WARSHIPS OF THE U.S. NAVY IN WORLD WAR TWO... 160 MILES FROM THE PACIFIC OCEAN ON THE COLUMBUS RIVER IN OREGON AT THE PORT OF HOOD RIVER...

U.S.S. 'INAUGRAL' (1944) (MSF 242).. A STEEL-HULLED MINESWEEPER OF WORLD WAR TWO VINTAGE AND NOW A FLOATING MUSEUM AT ST. LOUIS...

CMB-103... 70-FOOT COASTAL MOTOR BOAT PRESERVED AT H.M.S. 'DOLPHIN', GOSPORT, U.K. DELIVERED IN 1922, SHE REMAINED IN RESERVE UNTIL 1942. SHE SERVED IN THE CHANNEL AND AT NORMANDY, AND IS NOW A MEMORIAL TO COASTAL FORCES...

THE ROYAL NAVY COASTAL FORCES VETERANS ASSOCIATION HAS BOUGHT MTB-234 (UNTIL RECENTLY USED AS A HOUSEBOAT) TO BE RESTORED TO HER ORIGINAL WARTIME CONDITION AS A MUSEUM AT PORTSMOUTH...

ITALIAN 'MAS-15' (TORPEDO MOTOR LAUNCH) PRESERVED AT THE VITTORIANO MUSEUM IN ROME IN COMMEMORATION OF ITS FAMOUS AND SUCCESSFUL ATTACK ON THE AUSTRO-HUNGARIAN 'SZENT ISTVÁN' IN 1918 UNDER THE EQUALLY FAMOUS LT. CMDR. LUIGI RIZZO...

U.S. SUBMARINE MEMORIALS

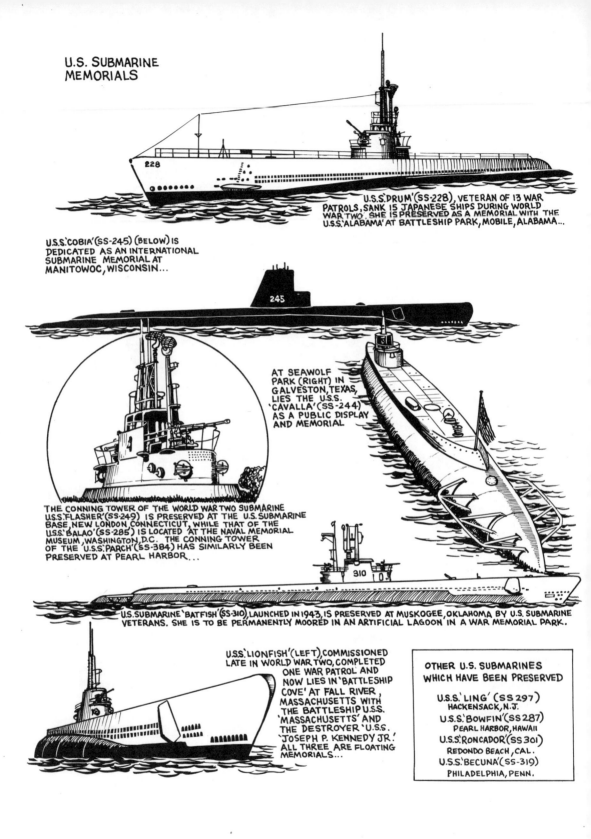

U.S.S. 'DRUM' (SS-228), VETERAN OF 13 WAR PATROLS, SANK 15 JAPANESE SHIPS DURING WORLD WAR TWO. SHE IS PRESERVED AS A MEMORIAL WITH THE U.S.S. 'ALABAMA' AT BATTLESHIP PARK, MOBILE, ALABAMA...

U.S.S. 'COBIA' (SS-245) (BELOW) IS DEDICATED AS AN INTERNATIONAL SUBMARINE MEMORIAL AT MANITOWOC, WISCONSIN...

AT SEAWOLF PARK (RIGHT) IN GALVESTON, TEXAS, LIES THE U.S.S. 'CAVALLA' (SS-244) AS A PUBLIC DISPLAY AND MEMORIAL

THE CONNING TOWER OF THE WORLD WAR TWO SUBMARINE U.S.S. 'FLASHER' (SS-249) IS PRESERVED AT THE U.S. SUBMARINE BASE, NEW LONDON CONNECTICUT, WHILE THAT OF THE U.S.S. 'BALAO' (SS-285) IS LOCATED AT THE NAVAL MEMORIAL MUSEUM, WASHINGTON, D.C. THE CONNING TOWER OF THE U.S.S. 'PARCH' (SS-384) HAS SIMILARLY BEEN PRESERVED AT PEARL HARBOR...

U.S. SUBMARINE 'BATFISH' (SS-310), LAUNCHED IN 1943, IS PRESERVED AT MUSKOGEE, OKLAHOMA BY U.S. SUBMARINE VETERANS. SHE IS TO BE PERMANENTLY MOORED IN AN ARTIFICIAL LAGOON IN A WAR MEMORIAL PARK.

U.S.S. 'LIONFISH' (LEFT), COMMISSIONED LATE IN WORLD WAR TWO, COMPLETED ONE WAR PATROL AND NOW LIES IN 'BATTLESHIP COVE' AT FALL RIVER, MASSACHUSETTS WITH THE BATTLESHIP U.S.S. 'MASSACHUSETTS' AND THE DESTROYER 'U.S.S. JOSEPH P. KENNEDY JR.' ALL THREE ARE FLOATING MEMORIALS...

OTHER U.S. SUBMARINES WHICH HAVE BEEN PRESERVED

U.S.S. 'LING' (SS 297)
HACKENSACK, N.J.
U.S.S. 'BOWFIN' (SS 287)
PEARL HARBOR, HAWAII
U.S.S. 'RONCADOR' (SS 301)
REDONDO BEACH, CAL.
U.S.S. 'BECUNA' (SS 319)
PHILADELPHIA, PENN.

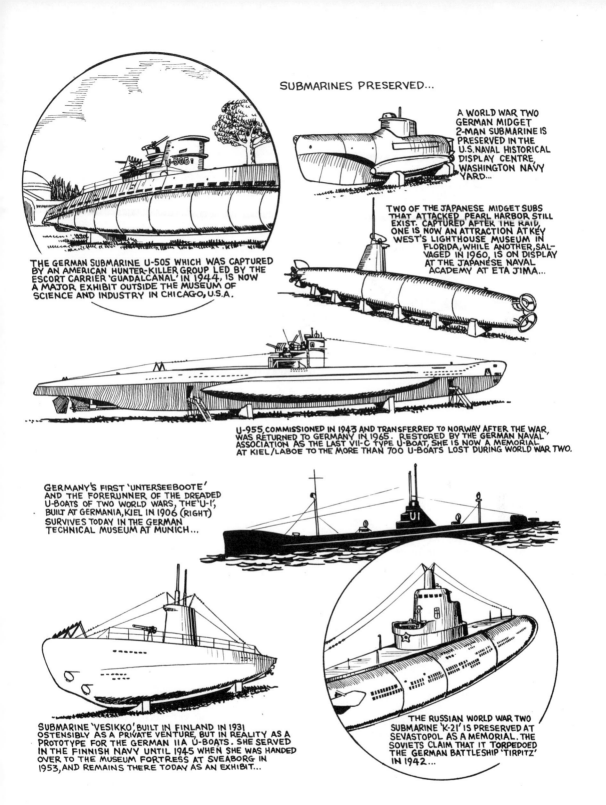

SUBMARINES PRESERVED...

A WORLD WAR TWO GERMAN MIDGET 2-MAN SUBMARINE IS PRESERVED IN THE U.S. NAVAL HISTORICAL DISPLAY CENTRE, WASHINGTON NAVY YARD...

THE GERMAN SUBMARINE U-505 WHICH WAS CAPTURED BY AN AMERICAN HUNTER-KILLER GROUP LED BY THE ESCORT CARRIER 'GUADALCANAL' IN 1944, IS NOW A MAJOR EXHIBIT OUTSIDE THE MUSEUM OF SCIENCE AND INDUSTRY IN CHICAGO, U.S.A.

TWO OF THE JAPANESE MIDGET SUBS THAT ATTACKED PEARL HARBOR STILL EXIST. CAPTURED AFTER THE RAID, ONE IS NOW AN ATTRACTION AT KEY WEST'S LIGHTHOUSE MUSEUM IN FLORIDA, WHILE ANOTHER, SALVAGED IN 1960, IS ON DISPLAY AT THE JAPANESE NAVAL ACADEMY AT ETA JIMA...

U-955, COMMISSIONED IN 1943 AND TRANSFERRED TO NORWAY AFTER THE WAR, WAS RETURNED TO GERMANY IN 1965. RESTORED BY THE GERMAN NAVAL ASSOCIATION AS THE LAST VII-C TYPE U-BOAT, SHE IS NOW A MEMORIAL AT KIEL/LABOE TO THE MORE THAN 700 U-BOATS LOST DURING WORLD WAR TWO.

GERMANY'S FIRST 'UNTERSEEBOOTE' AND THE FORERUNNER OF THE DREADED U-BOATS OF TWO WORLD WARS, THE 'U-1', BUILT AT GERMANIA, KIEL IN 1906 (RIGHT) SURVIVES TODAY IN THE GERMAN TECHNICAL MUSEUM AT MUNICH...

SUBMARINE 'VESIKKO' BUILT IN FINLAND IN 1931 OSTENSIBLY AS A PRIVATE VENTURE, BUT IN REALITY AS A PROTOTYPE FOR THE GERMAN IIA U-BOATS. SHE SERVED IN THE FINNISH NAVY UNTIL 1945 WHEN SHE WAS HANDED OVER TO THE MUSEUM FORTRESS AT SVEABORG IN 1953, AND REMAINS THERE TODAY AS AN EXHIBIT...

THE RUSSIAN WORLD WAR TWO SUBMARINE 'K-21' IS PRESERVED AT SEVASTOPOL AS A MEMORIAL. THE SOVIETS CLAIM THAT IT TORPEDOED THE GERMAN BATTLESHIP 'TIRPITZ' IN 1942...

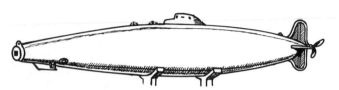

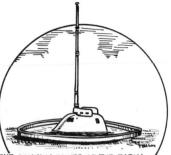

BUILT IN 1887, THE SPANISH SUBMARINE 'PERAL' WAS ONE OF THE FIRST OPERATIONAL SUBMARINES IN ANY NAVY. SHE IS STILL ON DISPLAY TODAY AT THE MAIN ENTRANCE OF THE NAVAL SCHOOL AT CARTAGENA...

THE CONNING TOWER OF THE EARLY DUTCH SUBMARINE 'LUCTOR ET EMERGO' (HMNS O-I) BUILT IN 1905 AND SCRAPPED IN 1920, IS PRESERVED AS A MEMORIAL AT THE SUBMARINE BARRACKS AT DEN HELDER

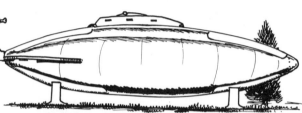

C.S.S. 'PIONEER' – THE OLDEST PRESERVED SUBMARINE IN THE WORLD, COMPLETED IN 1862 FOR THE CONFEDERATE NAVY. SCUTTLED TO PREVENT HER FALLING INTO UNION HANDS, SHE WAS LATER SALVAGED AND IS NOW LOCATED AT THE LOUISIANA STATE MUSEUM...

INVENTED IN 1879 BY J.P. HOLLAND, THE ONE-MAN SUBMARINE 'FENIAN RAM' SURVIVES TODAY AT PATERSON, NEW JERSEY. IT SANK DURING TRIALS AND WAS NOT RAISED UNTIL 1927...

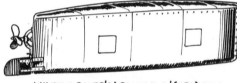

WILHELM BAUER'S 'PLONGEUR' (1850) WAS DESIGNED AS A PRIVATE VENTURE TO THREATEN THE DANISH BLOCKADE OF KIEL. SHE SANK DURING TRIALS BUT HER CREW ESCAPED, AND SHE WAS SUBSEQUENTLY SALVAGED AND DIS-PLAYED AT THE 'NAVAL SCHOOL AT KIEL...

THE EXPERIMENTAL SUB 'INTELLIGENT WHALE' WAS BUILT IN 1863 AND FINALLY SOLD TO THE U.S. NAVY IN 1869. SHE PROVED LESS THAN SUCCESSFUL. SHE WAS HAND-CRANKED BY SIX TO THIRTEEN MEN, AND IS NOW ON DISPLAY AT THE NAVAL MEMORIAL MUSEUM IN THE WASHINGTON ,D.C. NAVY YARD....

IN 1976-77, PLANS WERE IN HAND TO PRE-SERVE TWO BRITISH 'A' CLASS SUB-MARINES AS MUSEUMS. THEY ARE H.M. SUBMARINES 'ANDREW'(AT TORQUAY) AND 'ALLIANCE' (AT PORTSMOUTH)...

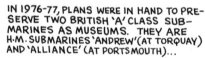

THE EARLY (1905) JAPANESE SUBMARINE 'SAKUMA NO.6' DISPLACED A MERE 57 TONS, AND WAS PLAGUED WITH ENGINE PROBLEMS. IN 1910 SHE SANK AFTER A PETROL EXPLOSION, BUT WAS RAISED AND REPAIRED. IN 1920 SHE BECAME A MEMORIAL AT KURE (LEFT)...

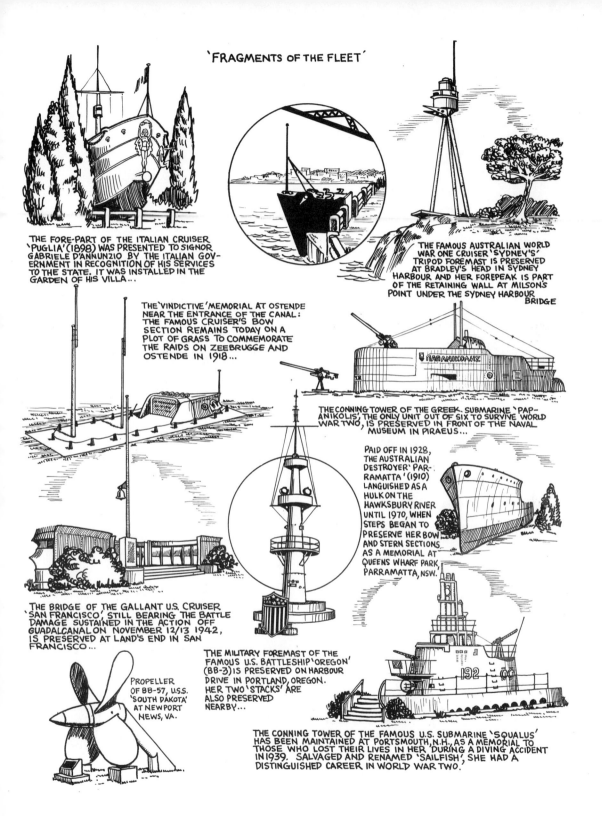

`FRAGMENTS OF THE FLEET`

THE FORE-PART OF THE ITALIAN CRUISER 'PUGLIA' (1898) WAS PRESENTED TO SIGNOR GABRIELE D'ANNUNZIO BY THE ITALIAN GOVERNMENT IN RECOGNITION OF HIS SERVICES TO THE STATE. IT WAS INSTALLED IN THE GARDEN OF HIS VILLA...

THE FAMOUS AUSTRALIAN WORLD WAR ONE CRUISER 'SYDNEY'S' TRIPOD FOREMAST IS PRESERVED AT BRADLEY'S HEAD IN SYDNEY HARBOUR AND HER FOREPEAK IS PART OF THE RETAINING WALL AT MILSON'S POINT UNDER THE SYDNEY HARBOUR BRIDGE

THE 'VINDICTIVE' MEMORIAL AT OSTENDE NEAR THE ENTRANCE OF THE CANAL: THE FAMOUS CRUISER'S BOW SECTION REMAINS TODAY ON A PLOT OF GRASS TO COMMEMORATE THE RAIDS ON ZEEBRUGGE AND OSTENDE IN 1918...

THE CONNING TOWER OF THE GREEK SUBMARINE 'PAPANIKOLIS', THE ONLY UNIT OUT OF SIX TO SURVIVE WORLD WAR TWO, IS PRESERVED IN FRONT OF THE NAVAL MUSEUM IN PIRAEUS...

PAID OFF IN 1928, THE AUSTRALIAN DESTROYER 'PARRAMATTA' (1910) LANGUISHED AS A HULK ON THE HAWKSBURY RIVER UNTIL 1970, WHEN STEPS BEGAN TO PRESERVE HER BOW AND STERN SECTIONS AS A MEMORIAL AT QUEENS WHARF PARK PARRAMATTA, NSW.

THE BRIDGE OF THE GALLANT U.S. CRUISER 'SAN FRANCISCO', STILL BEARING THE BATTLE DAMAGE SUSTAINED IN THE ACTION OFF GUADALCANAL ON NOVEMBER 12/13 1942, IS PRESERVED AT LAND'S END IN SAN FRANCISCO...

PROPELLER OF BB-57, U.S.S. 'SOUTH DAKOTA' AT NEWPORT NEWS, VA.

THE MILITARY FOREMAST OF THE FAMOUS U.S. BATTLESHIP 'OREGON' (BB-3) IS PRESERVED ON HARBOUR DRIVE IN PORTLAND, OREGON. HER TWO 'STACKS' ARE ALSO PRESERVED NEARBY...

THE CONNING TOWER OF THE FAMOUS U.S. SUBMARINE 'SQUALUS' HAS BEEN MAINTAINED AT PORTSMOUTH, N.H., AS A MEMORIAL TO THOSE WHO LOST THEIR LIVES IN HER DURING A DIVING ACCIDENT IN 1939. SALVAGED AND RENAMED 'SAILFISH', SHE HAD A DISTINGUISHED CAREER IN WORLD WAR TWO.'

35

HISTORIC NAVAL GUNS

THE 5.5-INCH GUN AT WHICH BOY CORNWELL WON HIS POSTHUMOUS V.C. ABOARD H.M.S. 'CHESTER' AT THE BATTLE OF JUTLAND, IS PRESERVED IN THE IMPERIAL WAR MUSEUM IN LONDON.

15-INCH GUNS FROM 'R' CLASS BATTLESHIPS 'RAMILLES' (RIGHT) AND 'RESOLUTION' (LEFT) UNVEILED IN FRONT OF THE IMPERIAL WAR MUSEUM IN LONDON IN 1968 AS RELICS OF THE 'BIG GUN ERA'.

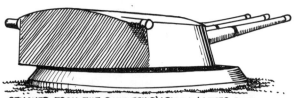

REMOVED FROM THE BATTLESHIP 'ARIZONA' AFTER SHE WAS SUNK AT PEARL HARBOR ON 7 DECEMBER 1941, HER TRIPLE 14-INCH GUN TURRETS WERE SITED ASHORE AS COAST DEFENCE BATTERIES FOR THE DEFENCE OF THE HAWAIIAN ISLANDS...

4-INCH/50 CAL. GUN NUMBER 'THREE' OF THE U.S. DESTROYER 'WARD' (D.D.139) FIRED THE FIRST AMERICAN SHOT IN ANGER IN WORLD WAR TWO AND SANK AN ENEMY SUBMARINE ON THE MORNING OF 7TH DECEMBER, 1941, IS ENSHRINED AS A WAR MEMORIAL ON THE GROUNDS OF THE STATE CAPITOL IN ST. PAUL, MINNESOTA, U.S.A.

THE LAST SUBMARINE DECK GUN IN THE ROYAL NAVY— THAT OF H.M.S. 'ANDREW'—PAID OFF IN 1975 AFTER 26 YEARS OF SERVICE, HAS BEEN PRESERVED AT THE SUBMARINE MUSEUM AT H.M.S. 'DOLPHIN', GOSPORT, ENGLAND....

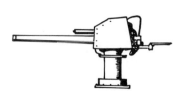

THE 4-INCH GUN FROM THE DESTROYER H.M.S. 'LANCE', WHICH FIRED THE FIRST BRITISH SHOT AT SEA IN THE GREAT WAR IS PRESERVED IN THE IMPERIAL WAR MUSEUM. H.M.S. 'LANCE', WITH HER SISTER H.M.S. 'LANDRALE', SANK THE GERMAN MINELAYER 'KÖNIGIN LUISE' ON 5th AUGUST, 1914...

5.9-INCH BATTERY GUN... VETERAN OF THE BATTLE OF JUTLAND AND THE ONLY REMAINING FRAGMENT OF THE GERMAN DREADNOUGHT 'OSTFRIESLAND' (1911)...

THE LAST RELICS OF THE 'MIGHTY HOOD'? TWO 5.5-INCH GUNS, SAID TO HAVE COME FROM H.M.S. 'HOOD'S SECONDARY BATTERY, AFTER HER 1940 REFIT, WERE MOUNTED ON ASCENSION ISLAND FOR COAST DEFENCE IN 1941. THEY REMAIN THERE TODAY. TWO OTHER 5.5-INCH GUNS, SIMILARLY PLACED AT TORSHAVN IN THE FAROES ISLANDS, AND ALSO SAID TO BE FROM H.M.S. 'HOOD', ARE ACTUALLY FROM THE CARRIER H.M.S. 'FURIOUS'...

...WHICH WAS EXPENDED AS A TARGET DURING BOMBING TESTS BY THE AMERICANS IN 1921. NOW LOCATED IN THE U.S. NAVAL MUSEUM, WASHINGTON NAVY YARD, WASHINGTON, D.C.

NAVAL REMNANTS...

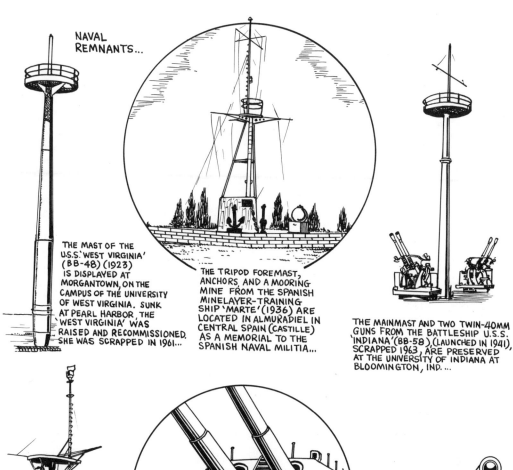

THE MAST OF THE U.S.S. 'WEST VIRGINIA' (BB-48) (1923) IS DISPLAYED AT MORGANTOWN, ON THE CAMPUS OF THE UNIVERSITY OF WEST VIRGINIA. SUNK AT PEARL HARBOR, THE 'WEST VIRGINIA' WAS RAISED AND RECOMMISSIONED, SHE WAS SCRAPPED IN 1961...

THE TRIPOD FOREMAST, ANCHORS, AND A MOORING MINE FROM THE SPANISH MINELAYER-TRAINING SHIP 'MARTE' (1936) ARE LOCATED IN ALMURADIEL IN CENTRAL SPAIN (CASTILLE) AS A MEMORIAL TO THE SPANISH NAVAL MILITIA...

THE MAINMAST AND TWO TWIN-40MM GUNS FROM THE BATTLESHIP U.S.S. 'INDIANA' (BB-58) (LAUNCHED IN 1941), SCRAPPED 1963, ARE PRESERVED AT THE UNIVERSITY OF INDIANA AT BLOOMINGTON, IND. ...

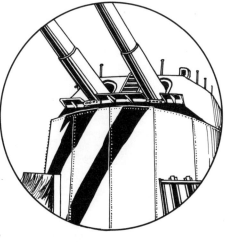

THE MAST AND OPEN BRIDGE OF THE HEAVY CRUISER U.S.S. 'PORTLAND' (CA-33) ARE DISPLAYED AT PORTLAND, MAINE, AS A MEMORIAL IN FORT ALLEN PARK. COMMISSIONED IN 1933, THE 'PORTLAND' SERVED THROUGHOUT THE PACIFIC WAR AND WAS SCRAPPED IN 1959...

AT THE JAPANESE MARITIME SELF DEFENCE FORCE COLLEGE AT ETAJIMA, A TWIN 14-INCH GUN TURRET IS DISPLAYED AS A REMINDER OF THE BATTLE-SHIP ERA AND THE FORMER IMPERIAL NAVY (ABOVE)...

THE TWO SIX-INCH DECK GUNS OF THE U.S. SUBMARINE 'NARWHAL' (SS-167) ARE ENSHRINED AT THE SUBMARINE BASE AT NEW LONDON, CONN. COMMISSIONED IN 1930, U.S.S. 'NARWHAL' SANK SEVEN JAPANESE SHIPS IN WORLD WAR TWO

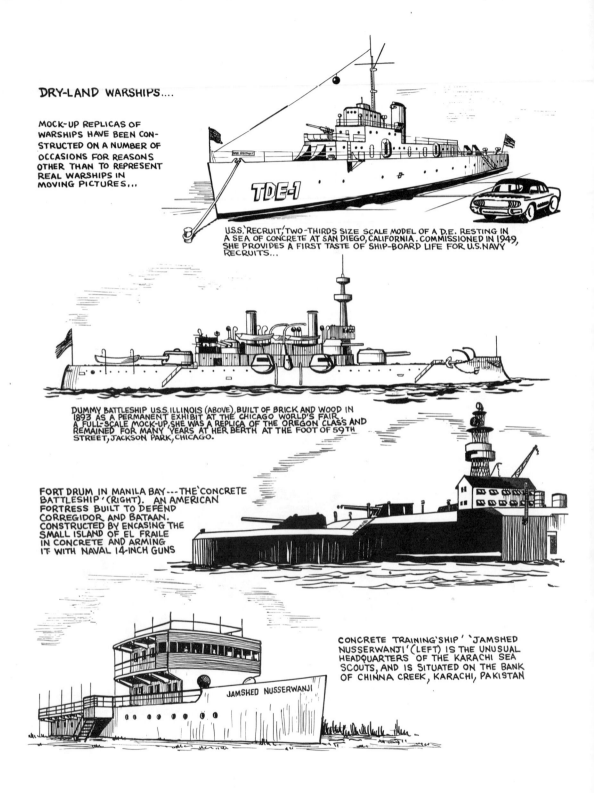

DRY-LAND WARSHIPS....

MOCK-UP REPLICAS OF
WARSHIPS HAVE BEEN CON-
STRUCTED ON A NUMBER OF
OCCASIONS FOR REASONS
OTHER THAN TO REPRESENT
REAL WARSHIPS IN
MOVING PICTURES...

TDE-1

U.S.S. 'RECRUIT' TWO-THIRDS SIZE SCALE MODEL OF A D.E. RESTING IN
A SEA OF CONCRETE AT SAN DIEGO, CALIFORNIA. COMMISSIONED IN 1949,
SHE PROVIDES A FIRST TASTE OF SHIP-BOARD LIFE FOR U.S. NAVY
RECRUITS...

DUMMY BATTLESHIP U.S.S. ILLINOIS (ABOVE), BUILT OF BRICK AND WOOD IN
1893 AS A PERMANENT EXHIBIT AT THE CHICAGO WORLD'S FAIR.
A FULL-SCALE MOCK-UP, SHE WAS A REPLICA OF THE OREGON CLASS AND
REMAINED FOR MANY YEARS AT HER BERTH AT THE FOOT OF 59TH
STREET, JACKSON PARK, CHICAGO.

FORT DRUM IN MANILA BAY --- THE 'CONCRETE
BATTLESHIP' (RIGHT).   AN AMERICAN
FORTRESS BUILT TO DEFEND
CORREGIDOR AND BATAAN.
CONSTRUCTED BY ENCASING THE
SMALL ISLAND OF EL FRAILE
IN CONCRETE AND ARMING
IT WITH NAVAL 14-INCH GUNS

CONCRETE TRAINING 'SHIP' 'JAMSHED
NUSSERWANJI' (LEFT) IS THE UNUSUAL
HEADQUARTERS OF THE KARACHI SEA
SCOUTS, AND IS SITUATED ON THE BANK
OF CHINNA CREEK, KARACHI, PAKISTAN

JAMSHED NUSSERWANJI

NAVAL MOCK-UPS

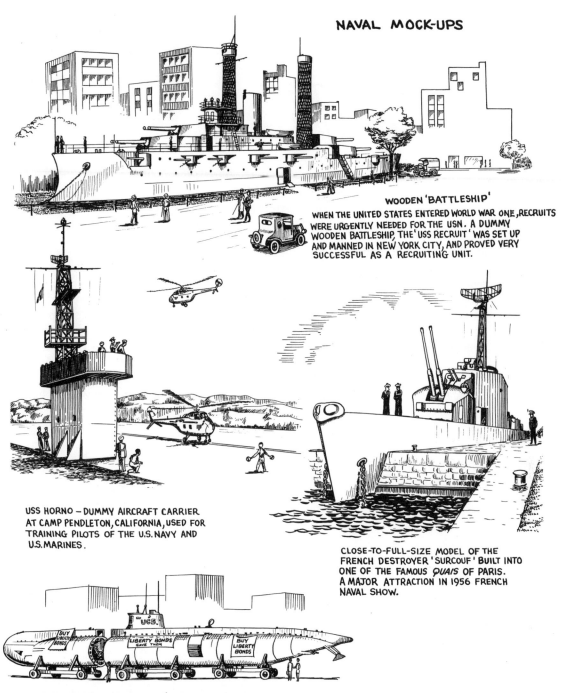

WOODEN 'BATTLESHIP'

WHEN THE UNITED STATES ENTERED WORLD WAR ONE, RECRUITS WERE URGENTLY NEEDED FOR THE USN. A DUMMY WOODEN BATTLESHIP, THE 'USS RECRUIT' WAS SET UP AND MANNED IN NEW YORK CITY, AND PROVED VERY SUCCESSFUL AS A RECRUITING UNIT.

USS HORNO — DUMMY AIRCRAFT CARRIER AT CAMP PENDLETON, CALIFORNIA, USED FOR TRAINING PILOTS OF THE U.S. NAVY AND U.S. MARINES.

CLOSE-TO-FULL-SIZE MODEL OF THE FRENCH DESTROYER 'SURCOUF' BUILT INTO ONE OF THE FAMOUS *QUAIS* OF PARIS. A MAJOR ATTRACTION IN 1956 FRENCH NAVAL SHOW.

SUBMARINE ON BROADWAY! IN 1917 THE GERMAN U-BOAT 'UC 5' WAS CAPTURED BY THE BRITISH, CUT INTO SECTIONS AND DRAWN THROUGH THE STREETS OF NEW YORK TO ADVERTISE LIBERTY BONDS!

PART THREE

WARSHIPS THAT MIGHT HAVE BEEN

MORE MAJOR warships have been scuttled by treaties, committees and bi-lateral agreements than were ever lost in battle. Because of financial cut-backs, changes of policy and the rapidity of international events, vast warship programmes have been wiped out by the stroke of a pen. Had some of the cancelled building programmes achieved completion, the entire balance of naval power would have been drastically altered, and the history of the first half of the twentieth century would probably have differed considerably from that which actually occurred.

Looking back at what is now a bygone age, it is interesting to examine the 'warships that might have been' and to speculate what might have happened had they been commissioned to carry out the dictates of their governments . . .

SHIPS THAT NEVER SAILED...
'CANCELLED CAPITAL SHIPS'

THE LAST PROJECTED BATTLESHIPS OF A DOOMED NAVY... THE AUSTRO-HUNGARIAN 'ERSATZ MONARCH' CLASS. THESE FOUR SHIPS WERE ORDERED IN 1914, BUT THE COURSE OF HISTORY DICTATED THEIR DEMISE AND THEY WERE NEVER LAID DOWN. THEY WOULD HAVE DISPLACED 25,000 TONS WITH A MAIN ARMAMENT OF TEN 13·8-INCH GUNS AND A SPEED OF 21 KNOTS...

FRENCH BATTLESHIP 'CLEMENCEAU' WAS LAID DOWN EARLY IN 1939 BUT WORK CEASED ON HER IN JUNE 1940. HER UNCOMPLETED HULL WAS FLOATED BY THE GERMANS AND SUNK BY ALLIED AIRCRAFT IN 1944. HAD SHE BEEN COMPLETED SHE WOULD HAVE BEEN ARMED WITH EIGHT 15-INCH GUNS IN TWO MASSIVE FOC'SL TURRETS...

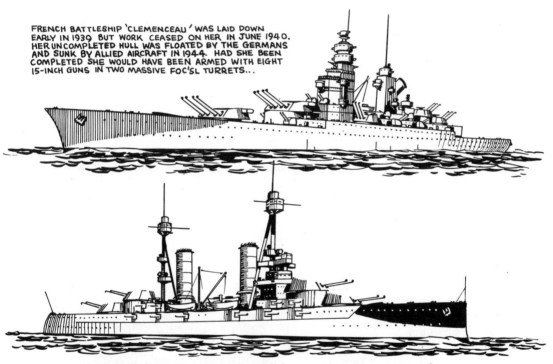

THE GREEK BATTLECRUISER 'SALAMIS' (LATER RENAMED 'VASSILEVS GEORGIOS') WAS TO HAVE BEEN THE ROYAL HELLENIC NAVY'S FIRST DREADNOUGHT CAPITAL SHIP. LAID DOWN IN GERMANY IN 1913, HER MAIN ARMAMENT OF EIGHT 14-INCH GUNS WAS ORDERED FROM THE BETHLEHEM STEEL CORPORATION OF AMERICA, WHILE HER SECONDARY 5·5-INCH GUNS WERE ORDERED FROM GREAT BRITAIN. THE OUTBREAK OF WAR IN 1914 PREVENTED HER COMPLETION, BUT HER AMERICAN-MADE GUNS WERE PURCHASED BY THE BRITISH AND MOUNTED ON THE ROYAL NAVY'S 'ABERCROMBIE' CLASS MONITORS. A SECOND CAPITAL SHIP WAS LAID DOWN IN A FRENCH YARD, BUT SIMILARLY CANCELLED IN 1914...

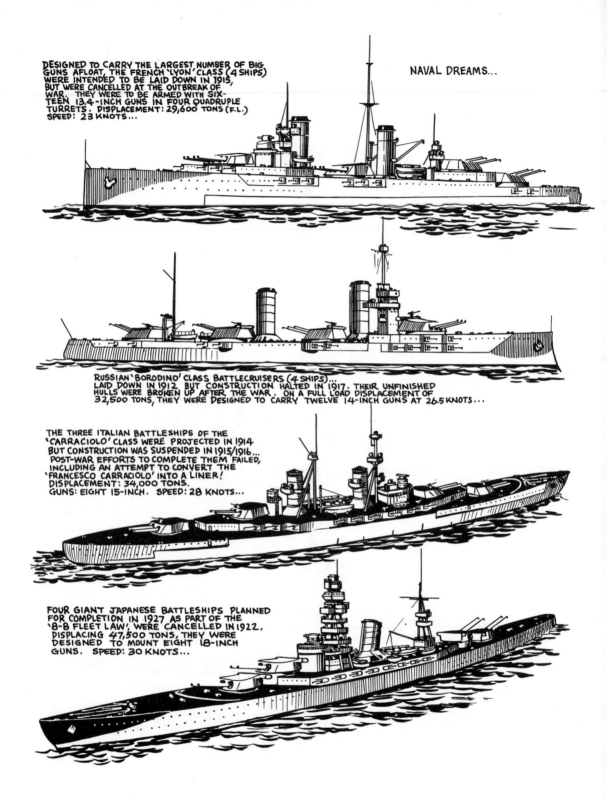

DESIGNED TO CARRY THE LARGEST NUMBER OF BIG
GUNS AFLOAT, THE FRENCH 'LYON' CLASS (4 SHIPS)
WERE INTENDED TO BE LAID DOWN IN 1915,
BUT WERE CANCELLED AT THE OUTBREAK OF
WAR. THEY WERE TO BE ARMED WITH SIX-
TEEN 13.4-INCH GUNS IN FOUR QUADRUPLE
TURRETS. DISPLACEMENT: 29,600 TONS (F.L.)
SPEED: 23 KNOTS...

NAVAL DREAMS...

RUSSIAN 'BORODINO' CLASS BATTLECRUISERS (4 SHIPS)...
LAID DOWN IN 1912 BUT CONSTRUCTION HALTED IN 1917. THEIR UNFINISHED
HULLS WERE BROKEN UP AFTER THE WAR. ON A FULL LOAD DISPLACEMENT OF
32,500 TONS, THEY WERE DESIGNED TO CARRY TWELVE 14-INCH GUNS AT 26.5 KNOTS...

THE THREE ITALIAN BATTLESHIPS OF THE
'CARRACIOLO' CLASS WERE PROJECTED IN 1914
BUT CONSTRUCTION WAS SUSPENDED IN 1915/1916...
POST-WAR EFFORTS TO COMPLETE THEM FAILED,
INCLUDING AN ATTEMPT TO CONVERT THE
'FRANCESCO CARRACIOLO' INTO A LINER!
DISPLACEMENT: 34,000 TONS.
GUNS: EIGHT 15-INCH. SPEED: 28 KNOTS...

FOUR GIANT JAPANESE BATTLESHIPS PLANNED
FOR COMPLETION IN 1927 AS PART OF THE
'8-8 FLEET LAW', WERE CANCELLED IN 1922.
DISPLACING 47,500 TONS, THEY WERE
DESIGNED TO MOUNT EIGHT 18-INCH
GUNS. SPEED: 30 KNOTS...

CANCELLED GIANTS...

FOUR MAGNIFICENT BATTLECRUISERS, KNOWN AS THE 'MACKENSEN' CLASS, WERE LAID DOWN BY GERMANY IN 1915, BUT THE DEMANDS OF THE GERMAN WAR INDUSTRY WERE SUCH THAT CONSTRUCTION WAS SUSPENDED IN 1917. HAD THEY BEEN COMPLETED, THEY WOULD HAVE CARRIED EIGHT 14-INCH GUNS ON A DISPLACEMENT OF 37,742 TONS (FULL LOAD) AT 27 KNOTS...

THREE FURTHER GERMAN BATTLECRUISERS DESIGNATED THE 'ERSATZ YORCK' CLASS WERE LAID DOWN IN 1916. LIKE THE 'MACKENSENS', CONSTRUCTION WAS HALTED ON THEM IN 1917. THEY WERE DESIGNED TO CARRY EIGHT 15-INCH GUNS ON A FULL-LOAD DISPLACEMENT OF 37,500 TONS. SPEED: 27.3 KNOTS...

THE FOUR BATTLECRUISERS OF THE JAPANESE 'AMAGI' CLASS WERE LAID DOWN IN 1920 AS PART OF THE '8-4' PROGRAMME, WHILE TWO MORE (KII CLASS) WERE ORDERED IN 1921. ALL WERE CANCELLED IN 1922 AS A RESULT OF THE WASHINGTON NAVAL TREATY, HOWEVER THE 'AKAGI' WAS COMPLETED AS AN AIRCRAFT CARRIER.
ARMAMENT: TEN 16-INCH GUNS.
DISPLACEMENT: 47,000 TONS (F.L.)
SPEED: 30 KNOTS...

THE TWO UNITS OF THE JAPANESE 'TOSA' CLASS WERE BATTLESHIP VARIATIONS OF THE 'AMAGIS' AND WERE ALSO LAID DOWN IN 1920 AND CANCELLED IN 1922, THOUGH THE 'KAGA' WAS COMPLETED AS AN AIRCRAFT CARRIER. THEIR ARMAMENT WAS TO BE TEN 16-INCH GUNS, DISPLACEMENT: 44,200 TONS (FULL LOAD), SPEED: 26.5 KNOTS...

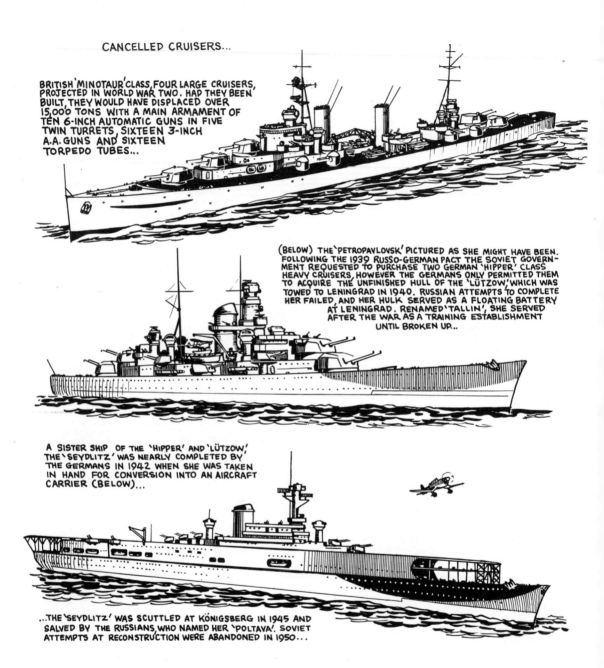

CANCELLED CRUISERS...

BRITISH 'MINOTAUR' CLASS, FOUR LARGE CRUISERS,
PROJECTED IN WORLD WAR TWO. HAD THEY BEEN
BUILT, THEY WOULD HAVE DISPLACED OVER
15,000 TONS WITH A MAIN ARMAMENT OF
TEN 6-INCH AUTOMATIC GUNS IN FIVE
TWIN TURRETS, SIXTEEN 3-INCH
A.A. GUNS AND SIXTEEN
TORPEDO TUBES...

(BELOW) THE 'PETROPAVLOVSK' PICTURED AS SHE MIGHT HAVE BEEN.
FOLLOWING THE 1939 RUSSO-GERMAN PACT THE SOVIET GOVERN-
MENT REQUESTED TO PURCHASE TWO GERMAN 'HIPPER' CLASS
HEAVY CRUISERS, HOWEVER THE GERMANS ONLY PERMITTED THEM
TO ACQUIRE THE UNFINISHED HULL OF THE 'LÜTZOW', WHICH WAS
TOWED TO LENINGRAD IN 1940. RUSSIAN ATTEMPTS TO COMPLETE
HER FAILED, AND HER HULK SERVED AS A FLOATING BATTERY
AT LENINGRAD. RENAMED 'TALLIN', SHE SERVED
AFTER THE WAR AS A TRAINING ESTABLISHMENT
UNTIL BROKEN UP...

A SISTER SHIP OF THE 'HIPPER' AND 'LÜTZOW',
THE 'SEYDLITZ' WAS NEARLY COMPLETED BY
THE GERMANS IN 1942 WHEN SHE WAS TAKEN
IN HAND FOR CONVERSION INTO AN AIRCRAFT
CARRIER (BELOW)...

...THE 'SEYDLITZ' WAS SCUTTLED AT KÖNIGSBERG IN 1945 AND
SALVED BY THE RUSSIANS, WHO NAMED HER 'POLTAVA'. SOVIET
ATTEMPTS AT RECONSTRUCTION WERE ABANDONED IN 1950...

SOVIET ASPIRATIONS

'SOVIETSKY SOYUZ' AND 'SOVIETSKAYA UKRAINA', GIANT BATTLESHIPS (65,000 TONS, FULL LOAD), LAID DOWN IN 1938 BUT HULLS ABANDONED IN 1940 DUE TO TECHNICAL AND MATERIAL DIFFICULTIES. MYSTERY SURROUNDS THEIR BRIEF HISTORY. SOME REPORTS CLAIMED THEY WERE TO BE MISSILE-ARMED, OTHERS THAT THEY HAD ONE FUNNEL ONLY. ARMAMENT INCLUDED NINE 16-INCH AND TWELVE 6-INCH GUNS. DESIGNED SPEED: 32 KNOTS...

THE FAST BATTLESHIPS 'STRANA SOVIETOV' AND 'SOVIETSKAYA BIELOROSSIYA' WERE LAID DOWN IN 1939. THEIR ITALIAN-INSPIRED DESIGN CALLED FOR A DISPLACEMENT OF 35,000 TONS AND THEIR EIGHT 15-INCH GUNS WERE ORDERED FROM GERMANY. NEEDLESS TO SAY, THEIR UNFINISHED HULLS WERE ABANDONED EARLY IN WORLD WAR TWO...

RUSSIAN 'KRONSTADT' AND 'SEVASTOPOL' BATTLE CRUISERS CONCEIVED TO COUNTER THE GERMAN 'SCHARNHORST' CLASS, WERE DESIGNED TO DISPLACE 38,360 TONS AND AT LEAST ONE WAS LAID DOWN PRIOR TO 1940. THEY WERE TO BE ARMED WITH NINE 12-INCH GUNS AND CAPABLE OF 33 KNOTS. LIKE THE OTHER SOVIET HEAVY SHIPS, THEY WERE ABANDONED EARLY IN THE WAR...

MYSTERY SURROUNDS THE PRECISE SPECIFICATIONS OF THE SOVIET SHIPS, AND THEIR APPEARANCE AND DETAILS ARE BASED ON CONJECTURE. A POST-WAR CLASS OF HEAVY CRUISERS, DESIGNATED THE 'STALINGRAD' CLASS, WAS ALSO PROJECTED, TO BE ARMED WITH NINE 12-INCH GUNS ... A SURPRISING PROJECT AFTER THE CANCELLATION OF THE 'KRONSTADTS'...

TWO JAPANESE BATTLECRUISERS WERE AUTHORIZED IN 1941 TO COUNTER THE U.S. 'ALASKA' CLASS, BUT WERE CANCELLED DUE TO PRESSING CONSTRUCTION PROBLEMS. DESIGNATED '795' AND '796', THEY WOULD HAVE DISPLACED 32,000 TONS, AND BEEN ARMED WITH NINE 12.2-INCH GUNS. SPEED: 33 KNOTS...

PART FOUR

SMALL BATTLE UNITS

FROM THE Confederate 'Davids' (small, manually-operated submersibles armed with spar torpedoes) of the American Civil War to the missile-armed Fast Patrol Boats of the late twentieth century, 'small battle units' have held a great attraction, particularly for smaller navies, because of their economy of development, acquisition, deployment and for the great destructive power of which they were capable – often far out of proportion to their diminutive size. These 'mini' units were largely developed by the Italians who were capable of great feats of individual gallantry and who employed them aggressively and effectively. Other countries were quick to take note and to develop their own 'small battle units'.

SMALL BATTLE UNITS

THE ITALIAN NAVY PIONEERED THE DEVELOPMENT AND SUCCESSFUL EMPLOYMENT OF MIDGET COMBATANTS IN BOTH WORLD WARS··· WEAPONS THAT RELIED UPON STEALTH AS MUCH AS HIGH EXPLOSIVE···

(ABOVE) ITALIAN 'BARCHNI SALTATORI' (JUMPING BOAT OR 'SEA TANK' DEVELOPED IN 1918 TO CRAWL OVER HARBOUR BARRAGES. SPIKED TRACKS WERE BOTH SIDES OF THE HULL. CREW: 4, TWO 17·7-INCH TORPEDOES. 4 KNOTS. FITTED ON ARMED WITH

BRITISH 55-FOOT COASTAL 'M.L.' (MOTOR LAUNCH) OF WORLD WAR ONE, ARMED WITH ONE OR TWO TORPEDOES, CARRIED AFT IN A TROUGH WHICH WERE LAUNCHED TAIL-FIRST OVER THE STERN. A 70-FOOT VERSION CARRIED FOUR MINES. SPEEDS VARIED TO 40 KNOTS···

ITALIAN 'MAS' (MOTOBARCA ARMATA SVAN)··· WORLD WAR ONE MOTOR LAUNCH (16 TONS, 25 KNOTS, TWO 17·7-INCH TORPEDOES.

ITALIAN ASSAULT BOAT (WORLD WAR TWO). ONE-MAN EXPLOSIVE LAUNCH THAT WAS AIMED LIKE A TORPEDO OR SET TO SINK BELOW ITS TARGET AND EXPLODE LIKE A MINE. THE PILOT ESCAPED BY RELEASING A FOLDING RAFT BEHIND THE COCKPIT···

JAPANESE 'SHINYO' SUICIDE BOAT (WORLD WAR TWO) WITH EXPLOSIVE CHARGE IN BOW AND TWO 5-INCH ANTI-PERSONNEL ROCKETS IN STERN. 6,000 WERE BUILT BUT THEIR EFFECT ON ALLIED SHIPPING WAS NEGLIGIBLE···

'CHARIOT'··· BRITISH VERSION OF THE ITALIAN TWO-MAN HUMAN TORPEDO. SPEED 3.5 KNOTS 700 LB. WARHEAD··· (WORLD WAR TWO)··· DESIGNED TO ATTACK SHIPS IN PROTECTED ANCHORAGES···

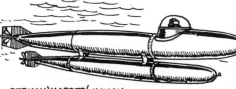

GERMAN 'MARDER' HUMAN TORPEDO (WORLD WAR TWO). THE PILOT CONTROLLED THE UPPER UNARMED 'TORPEDO' FROM WHICH WAS SLUNG A SECOND 21-INCH ARMED TORPEDO. THE ASSEMBLY COULD NOT COMPLETELY SUBMERGE, THE PILOT'S HEAD REMAINING ABOVE WATER. (ALSO CALLED A 'NEGER'. LATE-COMERS IN THE FIELD OF SMALL SUBMERSIBLES, THE GERMAN DESIGNS WERE HURRIEDLY PUT TOGETHER···

JAPANESE 'KAITEN' HUMAN SUICIDE TORPEDO (WORLD WAR TWO). A MODIFIED 'LONG LANCE' TORPEDO 54 FEET LONG WITH A 3,000 LB. WARHEAD. CARRIED TO WITHIN STRIKING RANGE OF ITS TARGET ON THE DECK OF A SUBMARINE, THE PILOT ENTERED HIS WEAPON THROUGH A CONNECTING TUBE FROM THE SUBMARINE'S HULL BEFORE STARTING HIS ONE-WAY MISSION···

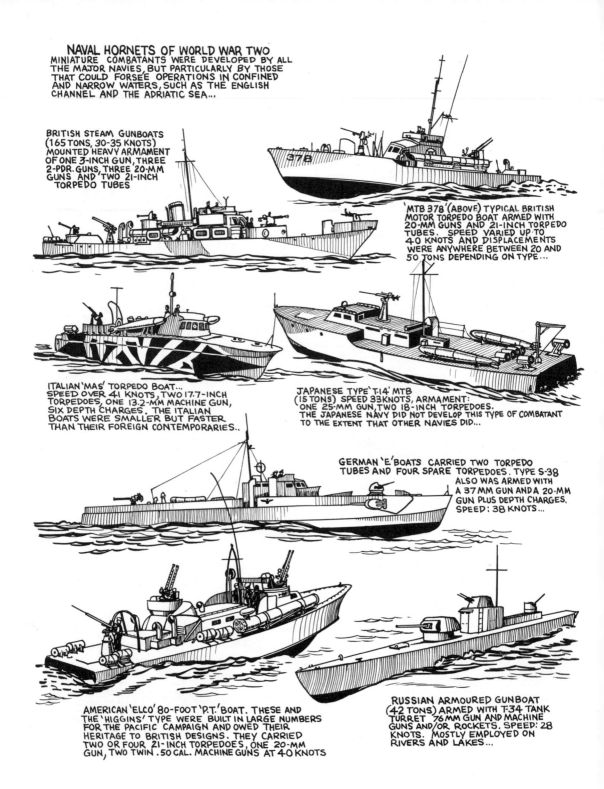

NAVAL HORNETS OF WORLD WAR TWO

MINIATURE COMBATANTS WERE DEVELOPED BY ALL THE MAJOR NAVIES, BUT PARTICULARLY BY THOSE THAT COULD FORSEE OPERATIONS IN CONFINED AND NARROW WATERS, SUCH AS THE ENGLISH CHANNEL AND THE ADRIATIC SEA...

BRITISH STEAM GUNBOATS (165 TONS, 30-35 KNOTS) MOUNTED HEAVY ARMAMENT OF ONE 3-INCH GUN, THREE 2-PDR. GUNS, THREE 20-MM GUNS AND TWO 21-INCH TORPEDO TUBES

'MTB 378' (ABOVE) TYPICAL BRITISH MOTOR TORPEDO BOAT ARMED WITH 20-MM GUNS AND 21-INCH TORPEDO TUBES. SPEED VARIED UP-TO 40 KNOTS AND DISPLACEMENTS WERE ANYWHERE BETWEEN 20 AND 50 TONS DEPENDING ON TYPE...

ITALIAN 'MAS' TORPEDO BOAT... SPEED OVER 41 KNOTS, TWO 17.7-INCH TORPEDOES, ONE 13.2-MM MACHINE GUN, SIX DEPTH CHARGES. THE ITALIAN BOATS WERE SMALLER BUT FASTER THAN THEIR FOREIGN CONTEMPORARIES..

JAPANESE TYPE 'T-14' MTB (15 TONS) SPEED 33KNOTS, ARMAMENT: ONE 25-MM GUN, TWO 18-INCH TORPEDOES. THE JAPANESE NAVY DID NOT DEVELOP THIS TYPE OF COMBATANT TO THE EXTENT THAT OTHER NAVIES DID...

GERMAN 'E' BOATS CARRIED TWO TORPEDO TUBES AND FOUR SPARE TORPEDOES. TYPE S-38 ALSO WAS ARMED WITH A 37MM GUN AND A 20-MM GUN PLUS DEPTH CHARGES, SPEED: 38 KNOTS...

AMERICAN 'ELCO' 80-FOOT 'P.T.' BOAT. THESE AND THE 'HIGGINS' TYPE WERE BUILT IN LARGE NUMBERS FOR THE PACIFIC CAMPAIGN AND OWED THEIR HERITAGE TO BRITISH DESIGNS. THEY CARRIED TWO OR FOUR 21-INCH TORPEDOES, ONE 20-MM GUN, TWO TWIN .50 CAL. MACHINE GUNS AT 40 KNOTS

RUSSIAN ARMOURED GUNBOAT (42 TONS) ARMED WITH T-34 TANK TURRET 76MM GUN AND MACHINE GUNS AND/OR ROCKETS. SPEED: 28 KNOTS. MOSTLY EMPLOYED ON RIVERS AND LAKES...

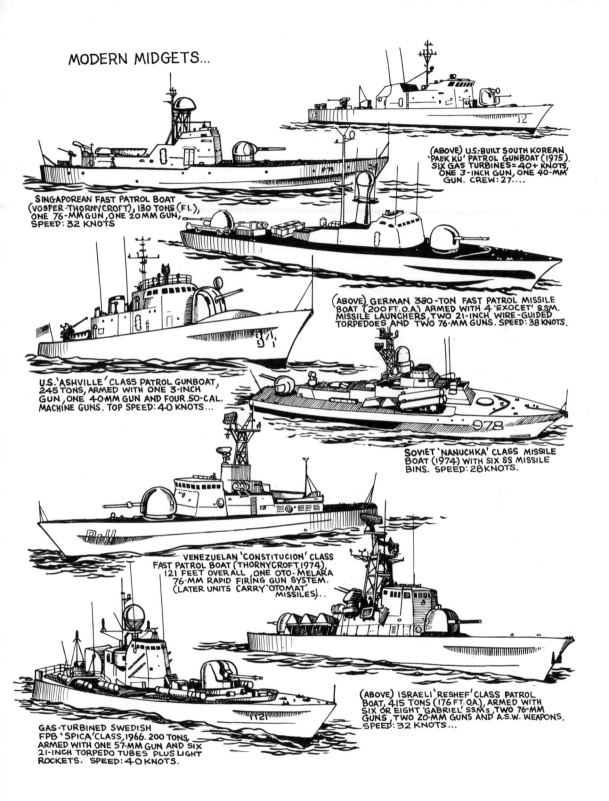

MODERN MIDGETS...

(ABOVE) U.S.-BUILT SOUTH KOREAN 'PAEK KU' PATROL GUNBOAT (1975). SIX GAS TURBINES = 40+ KNOTS, ONE 3-INCH GUN, ONE 40-MM GUN. CREW: 27....

SINGAPOREAN FAST PATROL BOAT (VOSPER-THORNYCROFT), 130 TONS (FL), ONE 76-MM GUN, ONE 20MM GUN, SPEED: 32 KNOTS

(ABOVE) GERMAN 380-TON FAST PATROL MISSILE BOAT (200 FT. O.A) ARMED WITH 4 'EXOCET' S.S.M. MISSILE LAUNCHERS, TWO 21-INCH WIRE-GUIDED TORPEDOES AND TWO 76-MM GUNS. SPEED: 38 KNOTS.

U.S. 'ASHVILLE' CLASS PATROL GUNBOAT, 245 TONS, ARMED WITH ONE 3-INCH GUN, ONE 40-MM GUN AND FOUR .50-CAL. MACHINE GUNS. TOP SPEED: 40 KNOTS...

SOVIET 'NANUCHKA' CLASS MISSILE BOAT (1974) WITH SIX SS MISSILE BINS. SPEED: 28 KNOTS.

VENEZUELAN 'CONSTITUCION' CLASS FAST PATROL BOAT (THORNYCROFT 1974). 121 FEET OVERALL, ONE OTO-MELARA 76-MM RAPID FIRING GUN SYSTEM. (LATER UNITS CARRY 'OTOMAT' MISSILES)...

(ABOVE) ISRAELI 'RESHEF' CLASS PATROL BOAT, 415 TONS (176 FT. O.A.), ARMED WITH SIX OR EIGHT 'GABRIEL' SSMs, TWO 76-MM GUNS, TWO 20-MM GUNS AND A.S.W. WEAPONS. SPEED: 32 KNOTS...

GAS-TURBINED SWEDISH FPB 'SPICA' CLASS, 1966. 200 TONS, ARMED WITH ONE 57-MM GUN AND SIX 21-INCH TORPEDO TUBES PLUS LIGHT ROCKETS. SPEED: 40 KNOTS.

MIDGET SUBMERSIBLES
THE ITALIAN NAVY EXPERIMENTED WITH TINY SUBMARINES AS
EARLY AS 1912 TO HELP DEFEND THEIR HARBOURS...

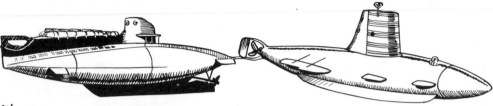

'A' TYPE ITALIAN FIRST WORLD WAR MIDGET
SUBMARINES WERE RAILWAY TRANSPORTABLE
AND HAD A CREW OF THREE. THEY CARRIED
TWO 17.7-INCH TORPEDOES IN EXTERIOR
DECK CAGES...

ITALIAN ONE-MAN EXPERIMENTAL SUBMARINE
BUILT IN THE VENICE NAVY YARD, 1912/13...

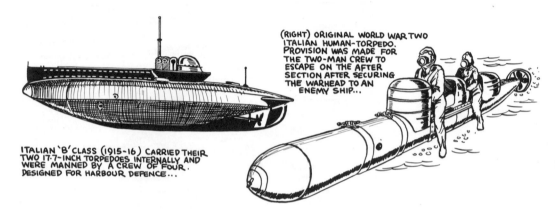

(RIGHT) ORIGINAL WORLD WAR TWO
ITALIAN HUMAN-TORPEDO.
PROVISION WAS MADE FOR
THE TWO-MAN CREW TO
ESCAPE ON THE AFTER
SECTION AFTER SECURING
THE WARHEAD TO AN
ENEMY SHIP...

ITALIAN 'B' CLASS (1915-16) CARRIED THEIR
TWO 17.7-INCH TORPEDOES INTERNALLY AND
WERE MANNED BY A CREW OF FOUR.
DESIGNED FOR HARBOUR DEFENCE...

(LEFT) LATER TYPE OF ITALIAN TWO-MAN
TORPEDO (ABOUT 1942). RANGE
WAS APPROXIMATELY 15 MILES...

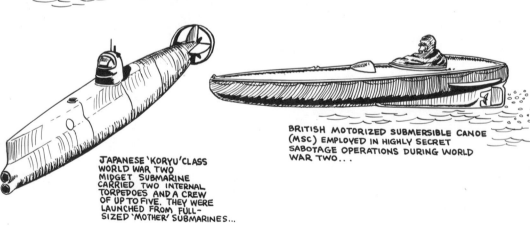

JAPANESE 'KORYU' CLASS
WORLD WAR TWO
MIDGET SUBMARINE
CARRIED TWO INTERNAL
TORPEDOES AND A CREW
OF UP TO FIVE. THEY WERE
LAUNCHED FROM FULL-
SIZED 'MOTHER' SUBMARINES...

BRITISH MOTORIZED SUBMERSIBLE CANOE
(MSC) EMPLOYED IN HIGHLY SECRET
SABOTAGE OPERATIONS DURING WORLD
WAR TWO...

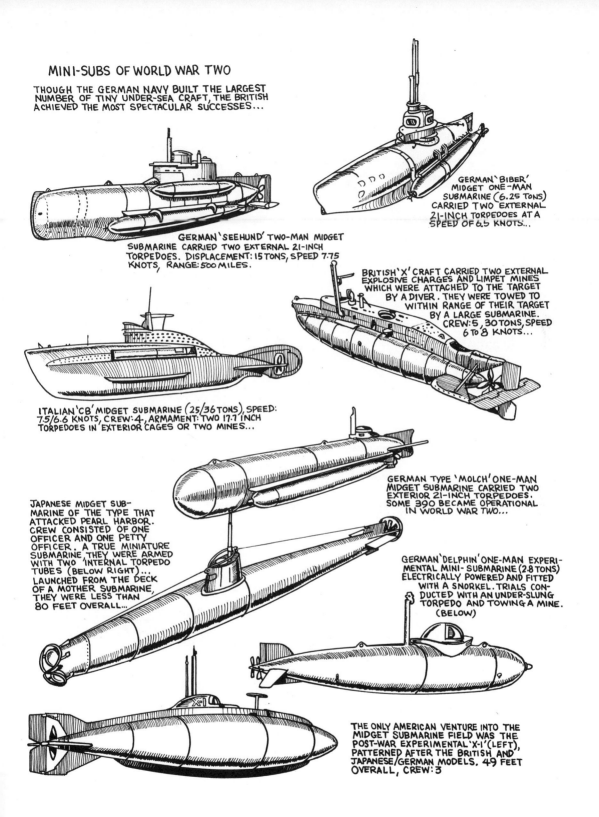

MINI-SUBS OF WORLD WAR TWO

THOUGH THE GERMAN NAVY BUILT THE LARGEST
NUMBER OF TINY UNDER-SEA CRAFT, THE BRITISH
ACHIEVED THE MOST SPECTACULAR SUCCESSES...

GERMAN 'SEEHUND' TWO-MAN MIDGET
SUBMARINE CARRIED TWO EXTERNAL 21-INCH
TORPEDOES. DISPLACEMENT: 15 TONS, SPEED 7.75
KNOTS, RANGE: 500 MILES.

GERMAN 'BIBER'
MIDGET ONE-MAN
SUBMARINE (6.25 TONS)
CARRIED TWO EXTERNAL
21-INCH TORPEDOES AT A
SPEED OF 6.5 KNOTS...

BRITISH 'X' CRAFT CARRIED TWO EXTERNAL
EXPLOSIVE CHARGES AND LIMPET MINES
WHICH WERE ATTACHED TO THE TARGET
BY A DIVER. THEY WERE TOWED TO
WITHIN RANGE OF THEIR TARGET
BY A LARGE SUBMARINE.
CREW: 5, 30 TONS, SPEED
6 TO 8 KNOTS...

ITALIAN 'CB' MIDGET SUBMARINE (25/36 TONS), SPEED:
7.5/6.6 KNOTS, CREW: 4, ARMAMENT: TWO 17.7 INCH
TORPEDOES IN EXTERIOR CAGES OR TWO MINES...

JAPANESE MIDGET SUB-
MARINE OF THE TYPE THAT
ATTACKED PEARL HARBOR.
CREW CONSISTED OF ONE
OFFICER AND ONE PETTY
OFFICER. A TRUE MINIATURE
SUBMARINE, THEY WERE ARMED
WITH TWO 'INTERNAL TORPEDO
TUBES (BELOW RIGHT)...
LAUNCHED FROM THE DECK
OF A MOTHER SUBMARINE,
THEY WERE LESS THAN
80 FEET OVERALL...

GERMAN TYPE 'MOLCH' ONE-MAN
MIDGET SUBMARINE CARRIED TWO
EXTERIOR 21-INCH TORPEDOES.
SOME 390 BECAME OPERATIONAL
IN WORLD WAR TWO...

GERMAN 'DELPHIN' ONE-MAN EXPERI-
MENTAL MINI-SUBMARINE (2.8 TONS)
ELECTRICALLY POWERED AND FITTED
WITH A SNORKEL. TRIALS CON-
DUCTED WITH AN UNDER-SLUNG
TORPEDO AND TOWING A MINE.
(BELOW)

THE ONLY AMERICAN VENTURE INTO THE
MIDGET SUBMARINE FIELD WAS THE
POST-WAR EXPERIMENTAL 'X-1' (LEFT),
PATTERNED AFTER THE BRITISH AND
JAPANESE/GERMAN MODELS. 49 FEET
OVERALL, CREW: 3

51

UNDERWATER MIDGETS...

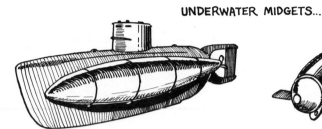

PAKISTANI 'SX404' CLASS MODERN MINI-SUBS, BUILT
IN ITALY IN 1972-73. DISPLACING 40 TONS, THEY HAVE
A CREW OF 4 AND CAN CARRY 12 PASSENGERS FOR
RAIDS ON HOSTILE SHORES. ALSO EMPLOYED FOR INSHORE
RECONNAISSANCE/INTELLIGENCE TASKS...

YUGOSLAV 'MALA' CLASS 2-MAN
FREE-FLOODING SUBMARINE
(1975).. ABOUT 25 FEET OVER-ALL.
EXPERIMENTAL CRAFT...

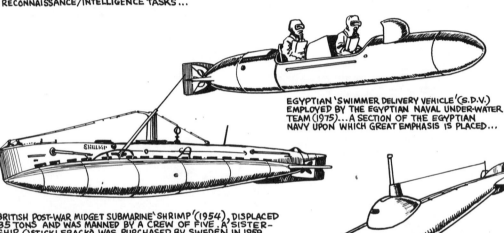

EGYPTIAN 'SWIMMER DELIVERY VEHICLE' (S.D.V.)
EMPLOYED BY THE EGYPTIAN NAVAL UNDER-WATER
TEAM (1975)... A SECTION OF THE EGYPTIAN
NAVY UPON WHICH GREAT EMPHASIS IS PLACED...

BRITISH POST-WAR MIDGET SUBMARINE 'SHRIMP' (1954), DISPLACED
35 TONS AND WAS MANNED BY A CREW OF FIVE. A 'SISTER-
SHIP ('STICKLEBACK') WAS PURCHASED BY SWEDEN IN 1958
AND BECAME THE 'SPIGGEN'. ANOTHER SISTER... 'SPRAT'
WAS TEMPORARILY LOANED TO THE U.S. NAVY IN 1958...

JAPANESE 'KAIRYU'
TYPE MIDGET SUBMARINE
(19+TONS), OF WHICH 213
WERE DELIVERED BY THE END
OF WWII. DESIGNED TO CARRY A
TORPEDO ON EITHER SIDE (OUTBOARD),
THEY WERE EMPLOYED AS SUICIDE
CRAFT WITH AN EXPLOSIVE CHARGE
IN THE NOSE...

MINI-CRUISERS

SEVERAL ATTEMPTS WERE MADE
BETWEEN THE WORLD WARS TO
ARREST THE EVER-INCREASING SIZE
OF NAVAL VESSELS, PARTICULARLY IN THE
CRUISER CATEGORY. FINANCIAL AND
TREATY RESTRICTIONS PRODUCED A
NUMBER OF EXAMPLES OF REDUCED
DISPLACEMENT WHILE AT THE
SAME TIME MAINTAINING CREDIBLE
ARMAMENT, SPEED, PROTECTION,
AND ENDURANCE...

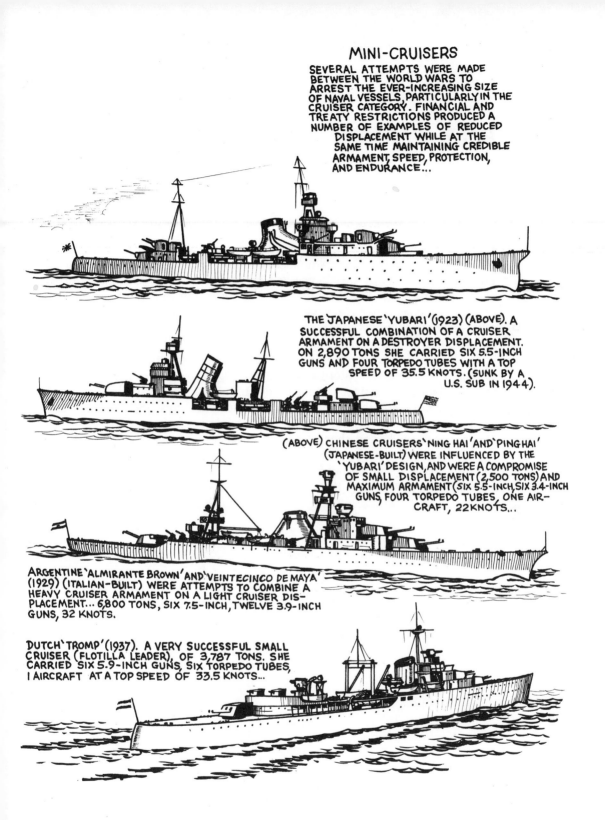

THE JAPANESE 'YUBARI' (1923) (ABOVE). A
SUCCESSFUL COMBINATION OF A CRUISER
ARMAMENT ON A DESTROYER DISPLACEMENT.
ON 2,890 TONS SHE CARRIED SIX 5.5-INCH
GUNS AND FOUR TORPEDO TUBES WITH A TOP
SPEED OF 35.5 KNOTS. (SUNK BY A
U.S. SUB IN 1944).

(ABOVE) CHINESE CRUISERS 'NING HAI' AND 'PING HAI'
(JAPANESE-BUILT) WERE INFLUENCED BY THE
'YUBARI' DESIGN, AND WERE A COMPROMISE
OF SMALL DISPLACEMENT (2,500 TONS) AND
MAXIMUM ARMAMENT (SIX 5.5-INCH, SIX 3.4-INCH
GUNS, FOUR TORPEDO TUBES, ONE AIR-
CRAFT, 22 KNOTS...

ARGENTINE 'ALMIRANTE BROWN' AND 'VEINTECINCO DE MAYA'
(1929) (ITALIAN-BUILT) WERE ATTEMPTS TO COMBINE A
HEAVY CRUISER ARMAMENT ON A LIGHT CRUISER DIS-
PLACEMENT... 6,800 TONS, SIX 7.5-INCH, TWELVE 3.9-INCH
GUNS, 32 KNOTS.

DUTCH 'TROMP' (1937). A VERY SUCCESSFUL SMALL
CRUISER (FLOTILLA LEADER), OF 3,787 TONS. SHE
CARRIED SIX 5.9-INCH GUNS, SIX TORPEDO TUBES,
1 AIRCRAFT AT A TOP SPEED OF 33.5 KNOTS...

PART FIVE

FOR THOSE IN PERIL . . .

NAUTICAL MISHAPS draw no distinction between war and peace. Year after year the tragic loss by mischance and misfortune is toted up. In time of war, because of the increased hazards and pressures, the rate climbs rapidly, but peacetime accidents to naval vessels, in spite of their highly-trained personnel and sophisticated equipment, are by no means a rarity, and some of the most costly naval disasters have occurred between the wars.

The majority of accidents at sea can be attributed to a small number of major causes. The elements — storms, fog, currents, etc. — are responsible for any number of mishaps, and the most extensive training coupled with the very latest in equipment have not eliminated them. Incompetence, misjudgement and faulty navigation cannot be ruled out as long as the human element is a factor, and these, together with uncharted shoals and inaccurate charts, will continue to imperil seamen for many years to come. Faulty equipment, and in time of war, mistaken identity, have led to numerous fatal errors, and not least of all have been the freaks of chance — or mischance — that have ended in tragic consequences.

...THE PERILS OF THE SEA...

A TERRIBLE HURRICANE STRUCK THE HARBOUR OF APIA, SAMOA ON 15-18 MARCH, 1889. RIDING AT ANCHOR WERE SEVEN WARSHIPS, H.M.S.'CALLIOPE', THE U.S. SHIPS 'TRENTON' AND 'VANDALIA', THE JAPANESE 'NIPSIC', THE RUSSIAN 'OLGA' AND THE GERMAN 'ADLER' AND 'EBER'. ALL OF THEM EXCEPT THE BRITISH SHIP BECAME TOTAL LOSSES. H.M.S.'CALLIOPE' WENT FULL AHEAD AND SLIPPED HER CABLE WHEN ONLY 6 FEET AWAY FROM A REEF...THE ONLY SHIP TO SURVIVE. 144 MEN WERE LOST ON THE AMERICAN AND GERMAN SHIPS. H.M.S.'CALLIOPE', A 16-GUN SINGLE SCREW CRUISER OF 2,770 TONS, WAS FINALLY PAID OFF EARLY IN WORLD WAR ONE...

ON 6TH SEPTEMBER, 1870, THE NEW BRITISH STEAM-DRIVEN ARMOURED SHIP H.M.S.'CAPTAIN', PROCEEDING ON HER MAIDEN VOYAGE ACROSS THE BAY OF BISCAY, ENCOUNTERED A FIERCE GALE. SHE HAD THE LOWEST FREEBOARD AND HEAVIEST MASTS IN THE FLEET, AND SHE FOUNDERED WITH A LOSS OF 490 LIVES, INCLUDING THAT OF HER DESIGNER. HER FAULTY DESIGN AND THE RESULTING CATASTROPHE LED TO CONSIDERABLE CONTROVERSY...

...THE SHIP THAT SANK TWICE! THE RUSSIAN COAST DEFENCE SHIP 'RUSALKA' HIT A SUBMERGED ROCK IN THE GULF OF FINLAND IN 1869 AND SANK, BUT WAS REFLOATED AND REPAIRED. ON 19TH SEPT. 1893 SHE FOUNDERED AGAIN IN A STORM IN THE GULF OF FINLAND WITH THE LOSS OF HER ENTIRE CREW.....

THE 18,000-TON U.S. ARMOURED CRUISER 'MEMPHIS' WAS STRUCK BY A MONSTER TIDAL WAVE WHILE LYING AT ANCHOR OFF SANTO DOMINGO ON THE 29TH AUGUST, 1916. SHE WAS DASHED ONTO A CORAL REEF AND WAS TOTALLY WRECKED WITH A LOSS OF 33 MEN...

THE UNITED STATES PADDLE-FRIGATE 'WATEREE' WAS THE VICTIM OF A GIANT TIDAL WAVE FOLLOWING AN EARTHQUAKE IN 1868. STRUCK BY THE HUGE WAVE WHILE PATROLLING OFF ARICA, CHILE, CLOSE TO THE PERUVIAN BORDER, SHE WAS HURLED THREE MILES INLAND! STRANGELY, SOME YEARS LATER, A SECOND EARTHQUAKE' CARRIED THE MAROONED HULK HALF WAY BACK AGAIN!

'DISASTERS EXECUTED'

ON 22 JUNE, 1893, THE BRITISH MEDITERRANEAN FLEET, UNDER ADMIRAL SIR GEORGE TYRON, WAS ENGAGED IN EVOLUTIONS. THE ADMIRAL ORDERED HIS TWO LINES OF BATTLESHIPS, WHICH WERE STEAMING ABREAST, TO REVERSE THEIR COURSE (180° TURN) BY TURNING INWARDS. THOUGH WARNED BY HIS OFFICERS THAT THERE WAS NOT SUFFICIENT DISTANCE BETWEEN THE SQUADRONS TO COMPLETE THE MANOEUVRE, THE ORDER WAS EXECUTED, AND THE FLAGSHIP, H.M.S.'VICTORIA', WAS RAMMED AND SUNK BY THE LEADING SHIP OF THE OTHER SQUADRON, H.M.S.'CAMPERDOWN', WITH A LOSS OF 359 LIVES, INCLUDING THAT OF THE ADMIRAL...

ON 8 SEPTEMBER, 1923 'DESTROYER SQUADRON 11' OF THE U.S. PACIFIC FLEET, LED BY THE U.S.S.'DELPHY', WAS STEAMING FROM 'SAN FRANCISCO TO SAN DIEGO, DOWN THE CALIFORNIA COAST IN THICK FOG. A MISCALCULATION BY THE LEADER, AS THE SQUADRON TURNED INTO THE SANTA BARBARA CHANNEL, RESULTED IN THE FIRST SEVEN SHIPS PILING UP ON THE VICIOUS ROCKS OF PERDERNALES POINT, ONE AFTER THE OTHER. THE U.S. NAVY LOST MORE FIGHTING SHIPS IN THIS ONE DISASTER THAN IT LOST DURING WORLD WAR ONE...

THE 'SCHARNHORST' WAS UNDOUBTEDLY THE MOST 'JINXED' SHIP IN THE NAZI NAVY. WHILE NEARING COMPLETION IN 1936 HER SCAFFOLDING COLLAPSED AND SHE ROLLED OVER, CRUSHING TO DEATH 61 WORKMEN, AND INJURING MANY MORE. THEN THE DAY BEFORE SHE WAS DUE TO BE LAUNCHED, SHE BROKE HER SECURING LINES AND LAUNCHED HERSELF, DESTROYING SEVERAL OTHER VESSELS IN THE PROCESS. RETURNING TO GERMANY AFTER SHE HAD SUSTAINED HEAVY DAMAGE WHILE BOMBARDING OSLO, SHE RAMMED AND SANK THE LINER 'BREMEN' (GERMANY'S LARGEST MERCHANT SHIP) IN AN UNACCOUNTABLE NAVIGATIONAL BLUNDER AT THE ENTRANCE TO THE ELBE. AFTER HER DAMAGE WAS REPAIRED A SUBSEQUENT FORAY ENDED UNDER THE GUNS OF H.M.S.'DUKE OF YORK' OFF NORTH CAPE, ON BOXING DAY, 1943...

STANDING INTO DANGER...

THE BRITISH BATTLESHIP H.M.S. 'MONTAGU' RAN INTO HEAVY FOG IN THE BRISTOL CHANNEL ON 29TH MAY, 1906 AFTER CONDUCTING WIRELESS EXERCISES. SHE GROUND ASHORE ON SHUTTER ROCK ON LUNDY ISLAND AND BECAME A TOTAL LOSS. HER BATTERED HULL REMAINS THERE TO THIS DAY...

THE 25,000-TON FRENCH DREADNOUGHT 'FRANCE' STRUCK AN UNCHARTED ROCK IN QUIBERON BAY ON 22nd. AUGUST, 1922. THE PINNACLE TORE HER BOTTOM OPEN FOR ONE THIRD OF HER LENGTH, AND SHE CAPSIZED FOUR HOURS LATER WITH A LOSS OF 3 MEN. THE IRONIC ASPECT OF THE DISASTER WAS THE FACT THAT QUIBERON BAY WAS A MUCH-FREQUENTED ANCHORAGE OF THE FRENCH FLEET...

THE BRITISH CRUISER 'RALEIGH', FLAGSHIP OF THE AMERICA AND WEST INDIES STATION IN 1922, WENT AGROUND IN THE STRAITS OF BELLE ISLE IN DENSE FOG AND BECAME A TOTAL LOSS. A PREDECESSOR, THE 50-GUN FRIGATE 'RALEIGH' WAS LOST IN SIMILAR CIRCUMSTANCES NEAR HONG KONG IN 1857

ON THE 12TH OF JUNE 1897, THE SMALL RUSSIAN BATTLESHIP 'GAGNUT' LED THE BALTIC TRAINING SQUADRON INTO THE GULF OF FINLAND FOR GUNNERY EXERCISES. OFF VIBORG, FINLAND, SHE STRUCK AN UNCHARTED ROCK WHICH RIPPED A LARGE GASH IN HER BOTTOM. FORTUNATELY, SHE SETTLED SLOWLY AND HER ENTIRE CREW ESCAPED BEFORE SHE SANK...

IN 1923 THE 15,000-TON SPANISH BATTLESHIP 'ESPANA' STRUCK AN UNCHARTED REEF OFF THE MOROCCAN RIFF COAST IN THICK FOG, AND FOUNDERED. THERE WAS SOME SUSPICION THAT SHE HAD STRUCK A DRIFTING MINE OF REPUBLICAN ORIGIN...

COSTLY COLLISIONS...

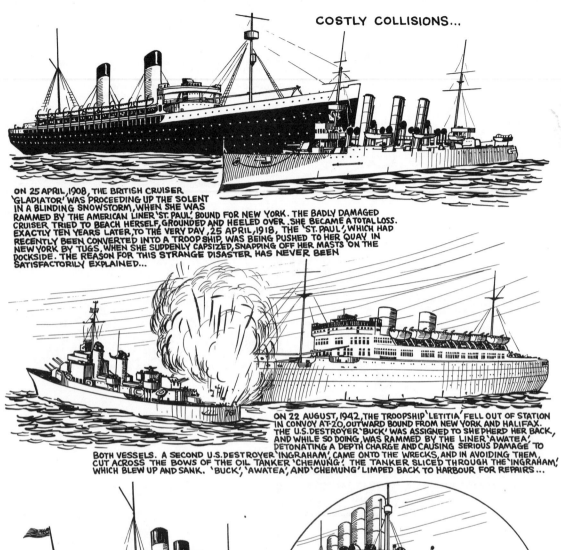

ON 25 APRIL, 1908, THE BRITISH CRUISER 'GLADIATOR' WAS PROCEEDING UP THE SOLENT IN A BLINDING SNOWSTORM, WHEN SHE WAS RAMMED BY THE AMERICAN LINER 'ST. PAUL', BOUND FOR NEW YORK. THE BADLY DAMAGED CRUISER TRIED TO BEACH HERSELF, GROUNDED AND HEELED OVER. SHE BECAME A TOTAL LOSS. EXACTLY TEN YEARS LATER, TO THE VERY DAY, 25 APRIL, 1918, THE 'ST. PAUL', WHICH HAD RECENTLY BEEN CONVERTED INTO A TROOP SHIP, WAS BEING PUSHED TO HER QUAY IN NEW YORK BY TUGS, WHEN SHE SUDDENLY CAPSIZED, SNAPPING OFF HER MASTS ON THE DOCKSIDE. THE REASON FOR THIS STRANGE DISASTER HAS NEVER BEEN SATISFACTORILY EXPLAINED...

ON 22 AUGUST, 1942, THE TROOPSHIP 'LETITIA' FELL OUT OF STATION IN CONVOY AT-20, OUTWARD BOUND FROM NEW YORK AND HALIFAX. THE U.S. DESTROYER 'BUCK' WAS ASSIGNED TO SHEPHERD HER BACK, AND WHILE SO DOING, WAS RAMMED BY THE LINER 'AWATEA', DETONATING A DEPTH CHARGE AND CAUSING SERIOUS DAMAGE TO BOTH VESSELS. A SECOND U.S. DESTROYER 'INGRAHAM', CAME ONTO THE WRECKS, AND IN AVOIDING THEM, CUT ACROSS THE BOWS OF THE OIL TANKER 'CHEMUNG'. THE TANKER SLICED THROUGH THE 'INGRAHAM', WHICH BLEW UP AND SANK. 'BUCK', 'AWATEA', AND 'CHEMUNG' LIMPED BACK TO HARBOUR FOR REPAIRS...

ON 20TH SEPTEMBER, 1911, THE GIANT WHITE STAR LINER 'OLYMPIC' WAS RAMMED BY THE BRITISH CRUISER 'HAWKE' IN THE ENGLISH CHANNEL AS THE TWO SHIPS WERE ATTEMPTING TO PASS EACH OTHER AT THE ENTRANCE TO THE SPITHEAD CHANNEL. THIS NAVIGATIONAL BLUNDER WAS NEVER SATISFACTORILY SETTLED...

WHILE ESCORTING THE BRITISH TRANSPORT 'AQUITANIA' IN THE ENGLISH CHANNEL ON 9TH OCTOBER, 1918, THE U.S. DESTROYER 'SHAW' WAS UNABLE TO COMPLETE A ZIG ZAG DUE TO A STEERING BREAKDOWN, AND THE GIANT LINER, WITH 8,000 TROOPS ABOARD, CUT THROUGH HER AT 26 KNOTS. AMAZINGLY, THE SHATTERED WRECK REACHED PORTSMOUTH, ENGLAND, WHERE A NEW BOW SECTION WAS FITTED...

NAVAL DISASTERS...

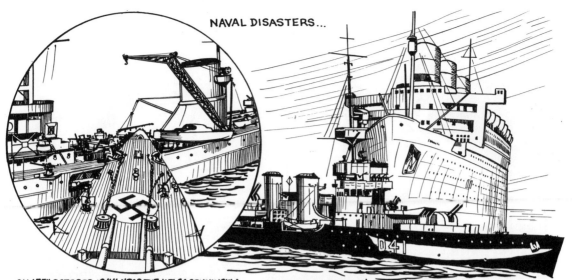

ON 15TH OCTOBER, 1944, NEAR THE HELGA PENNINSULA IN THE BALTIC SEA, THE GERMAN HEAVY CRUISER 'PRINZ EUGEN' RAMMED THE LIGHT CRUISER 'LEIPZIG', NEARLY SLICING HER IN TWO. 27 GERMAN SAILORS DIED, AND THE 'LEIPZIG' WAS RENDERED USELESS FOR THE REST OF THE WAR...

THE BRITISH 'A.A. CRUISER 'CURACOA' WAS SLICED IN TWO BY THE GIANT TROOP-CARRYING LINER 'QUEEN MARY' OFF BLOODY FORELAND, IRELAND, ENROUTE TO BRITAIN ON 2nd OCTOBER, 1942. MANY OF THE 15,000 U.S. TROOPS ONBOARD THE 'QUEEN MARY' WERE UNAWARE OF THE TRAGEDY. 'CURACOA' SANK RAPIDLY WITH HEAVY LOSS OF LIFE...

H.M.C.S. 'FRASER'S REPLACEMENT, H.M.C.S. 'MARGAREE' (EX-H.M.S. 'DIANA') SHARED HER PREDECESSOR'S FATE. SHE TOO WAS SUNK WHEN RAMMED ACCIDENTALLY BY THE FREIGHTER 'PORT FAIRY' ON 22 OCTOBER, 1940 IN THE NORTH ATLANTIC WITH A LOSS OF 140 LIVES...

EARLY IN WORLD WAR TWO, THE BRITISH A.A. CRUISER 'CALCUTTA' AND THE CANADIAN DESTROYER 'FRASER' WERE PART OF A FORCE OPERATING IN THE BAY OF BISCAY. A SERIES OF MANOEUVRES ORDERED BY H.M.S. 'CALCUTTA' CAUSED SOME CONFUSION, RESULTING IN A COLLISION IN WHICH THE CRUISER SLICED THE DESTROYER IN TWO. 'FRASER'S FORE PART DRIFTED AWAY, HER STERN SECTION REMAINED AFLOAT AND 60 SURVIVORS WERE TAKEN OFF BEFORE IT WAS SCUTTLED. HER ENTIRE BRIDGE WORKS ENDED UP 'SITTING' ON THE CRUISER'S FOC'SL!

THE BATTLESHIP 'BARHAM' ACCOMPANIED BY H.M.S. 'ARK ROYAL', RAMMED THE DESTROYER 'DUCHESS' IN THE CLYDE DURING WINTER DARKNESS ON 12TH DECEMBER, 1940. H.M.S. 'DUCHESS' ROLLED OVER AND SANK. THERE WERE ONLY 23 SURVIVORS OUT OF A CREW OF 140. ONE WEEK LATER THE 'BARHAM' WAS TORPEDOED AND DAMAGED BY U-30 OFF THE HEBRIDES..

IN THICK WEATHER ON 1ST MAY, 1942, WHILE COVERING MURMANSK CONVOY PQ 15, THE BRITISH DESTROYER 'PUNJABI' COLLIDED WITH THE BATTLESHIP 'KING GEORGE V'. THE DESTROYER SANK RAPIDLY, AND HER EXPLODING DEPTH CHARGES SERIOUSLY DAMAGED THE BATTLESHIP...

COSTLY COLLISIONS...

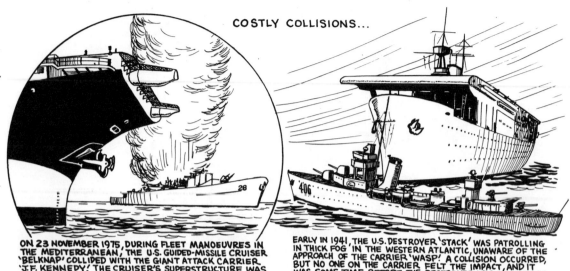

ON 23 NOVEMBER 1975, DURING FLEET MANOEUVRES IN THE MEDITERRANEAN, THE U.S. GUIDED-MISSILE CRUISER 'BELKNAP' COLLIDED WITH THE GIANT ATTACK CARRIER 'J.F. KENNEDY'! THE CRUISER'S SUPERSTRUCTURE WAS ALMOST ENTIRELY SHEARED OFF, AND HER SMOLDERING HULK WAS TOWED TO PRIOLO, SICILY THE NEXT DAY...

EARLY IN 1941, THE U.S. DESTROYER 'STACK' WAS PATROLLING IN THICK FOG IN THE WESTERN ATLANTIC, UNAWARE OF THE APPROACH OF THE CARRIER 'WASP'! A COLLISION OCCURRED, BUT NO ONE ON THE CARRIER FELT THE IMPACT, AND IT WAS SOME TIME BEFORE THE DESTROYER WAS DISCOVERED IMPALED ON THE CARRIER'S BOWS!... BEING DRIVEN SIDEWAYS THROUGH THE WATER! 'STACK' WAS EVENTUALLY REPAIRED. ODDLY ENOUGH, THE NEXT U.S.S.'WASP' SLICED THROUGH THE DESTROYER U.S.S.'HOBSON' IN ALMOST IDENTICAL WATERS TEN YEARS LATER!

AT THE CONCLUSION OF EXERCISES ON 6TH FEBRUARY, 1964, THE AUSTRALIAN DESTROYER 'VOYAGER' INEXPLICABLY ATTEMPTED TO CUT ACROSS THE BOWS OF THE CARRIER 'MELBOURNE'! CUT IN TWO, HER TWO HALVES SCRAPED DOWN BOTH SIDES OF THE CARRIER, AND SANK. THE DESTROYER'S CAPTAIN DID NOT SURVIVE TO EXPLAIN HIS ACTIONS. FIVE YEARS LATER, ON 3 JUNE, 1969, DURING SEATO EXERCISES, AND IN SIMILAR CIRCUMSTANCES, THE 'MELBOURNE' KNIFED THE U.S. DESTROYER 'FRANK E. EVANS' IN HALF, AND 74 U.S. SAILORS WERE LOST. THE CARRIER WAS INVOLVED IN A THIRD COLLISION ON 12 JULY, 1974, WHEN SHE COLLIDED WITH A LINER!

ON THE 9TH OF NOVEMBER, 1970, A RUSSIAN 'KOTLIN' CLASS DESTROYER, WHICH HAD BEEN HARASSING H.M.S.'ARK ROYAL' DURING MANOEUVRES IN THE MEDITERRANEAN, FINALLY DREW TOO CLOSE TO THE BRITISH CARRIER, AND IN THE RESULTING COLLISION, SUFFERED A DAMAGED AFTER SUPERSTRUCTURE AND THE LOSS OF TWO MEN....

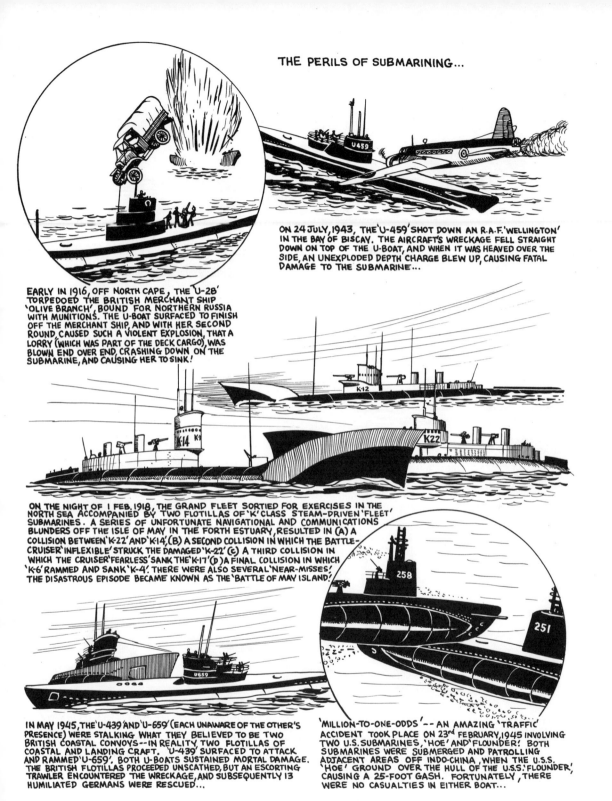

THE PERILS OF SUBMARINING...

ON 24 JULY, 1943, THE 'U-459' SHOT DOWN AN R.A.F. 'WELLINGTON' IN THE BAY OF BISCAY. THE AIRCRAFT'S WRECKAGE FELL STRAIGHT DOWN ON TOP OF THE U-BOAT, AND WHEN IT WAS HEAVED OVER THE SIDE, AN UNEXPLODED DEPTH CHARGE BLEW UP, CAUSING FATAL DAMAGE TO THE SUBMARINE...

EARLY IN 1916, OFF NORTH CAPE, THE 'U-28' TORPEDOED THE BRITISH MERCHANT SHIP 'OLIVE BRANCH', BOUND FOR NORTHERN RUSSIA WITH MUNITIONS. THE U-BOAT SURFACED TO FINISH OFF THE MERCHANT SHIP, AND WITH HER SECOND ROUND, CAUSED SUCH A VIOLENT EXPLOSION, THAT A LORRY (WHICH WAS PART OF THE DECK CARGO), WAS BLOWN END OVER END, CRASHING DOWN ON THE SUBMARINE, AND CAUSING HER TO SINK!

ON THE NIGHT OF 1 FEB. 1918, THE GRAND FLEET SORTIED FOR EXERCISES IN THE NORTH SEA ACCOMPANIED BY TWO FLOTILLAS OF 'K' CLASS STEAM-DRIVEN 'FLEET' SUBMARINES. A SERIES OF UNFORTUNATE NAVIGATIONAL AND COMMUNICATIONS BLUNDERS OFF THE ISLE OF MAY IN THE FORTH ESTUARY, RESULTED IN (A) A COLLISION BETWEEN 'K-22' AND 'K-14', (B) A SECOND COLLISION IN WHICH THE BATTLE-CRUISER 'INFLEXIBLE' STRUCK THE DAMAGED 'K-22' (C) A THIRD COLLISION IN WHICH THE CRUISER 'FEARLESS' SANK THE 'K-17' (D) A FINAL COLLISION IN WHICH 'K-6' RAMMED AND SANK 'K-4'. THERE WERE ALSO SEVERAL 'NEAR-MISSES'. THE DISASTROUS EPISODE BECAME KNOWN AS THE 'BATTLE OF MAY ISLAND'.

IN MAY 1945, THE 'U-439' AND 'U-659' (EACH UNAWARE OF THE OTHER'S PRESENCE) WERE STALKING WHAT THEY BELIEVED TO BE TWO BRITISH COASTAL CONVOYS -- IN REALITY TWO FLOTILLAS OF COASTAL AND LANDING CRAFT. 'U-439' SURFACED TO ATTACK AND RAMMED 'U-659'. BOTH U-BOATS SUSTAINED MORTAL DAMAGE. THE BRITISH FLOTILLAS PROCEEDED UNSCATHED, BUT AN ESCORTING TRAWLER ENCOUNTERED THE WRECKAGE, AND SUBSEQUENTLY 13 HUMILIATED GERMANS WERE RESCUED...

'MILLION-TO-ONE-ODDS' -- AN AMAZING 'TRAFFIC' ACCIDENT TOOK PLACE ON 23rd FEBRUARY, 1945 INVOLVING TWO U.S. SUBMARINES, 'HOE' AND 'FLOUNDER'! BOTH SUBMARINES WERE SUBMERGED AND PATROLLING ADJACENT AREAS OFF INDO-CHINA, WHEN THE U.S.S. 'HOE' GROUND OVER THE HULL OF THE U.S.S. 'FLOUNDER', CAUSING A 25-FOOT GASH. FORTUNATELY, THERE WERE NO CASUALTIES IN EITHER BOAT...

FRIENDLY ENEMIES....

THE BRITISH MINESWEEPING SLOOP H.M.S. 'HUSSAR' WAS BOMBED AND SUNK IN ERROR BY ALLIED AIRCRAFT OFF NORMANDY ON 27TH AUGUST, 1944...

THERE WERE MANY CASES OF SUBMARINES BEING ATTACKED BY THEIR OWN SIDE IN WORLD WAR TWO. THE RUSSIAN 'B-1' (EX-H.M.S. 'SUNFISH') WAS SUNK BY BRITISH AIRCRAFT ENROUTE TO RUSSIA, WHILE THE POLISH SUBMARINE 'JASTRZAB' (EX-R.N. P-551) WAS DEPTH-CHARGED BY BRITISH SURFACE UNITS OFF NORWAY IN 1942. THE SUBMARINE H.M.S. 'OXLEY' WAS RAMMED IN ERROR BY H.M. SUBMARINE 'TRITON' AND BOTH H.M. SUBMARINES 'P-514' AND 'UMPIRE' WERE RAMMED AND SUNK BY COMMONWEALTH SURFACE UNITS...

THE GERMAN DESTROYERS 'LEBERECHT MAASS' AND 'MAX SCHULTZ' WERE SUNK IN THE NORTH SEA ON 22nd. FEBRUARY, 1940 BY THE LUFTWAFFE, WHO HAD MISTAKEN THEM FOR BRITISH DESTROYERS. SIX MONTHS EARLIER, THE JINXED 'MAX SCHULTZ' HAD SUNK THE GERMAN TORPEDO BOAT 'TIGER' IN A COLLISION OFF BORNHOLM...

ON 17 SEPTEMBER, 1941, THE SWEDISH DESTROYERS 'GOTEBORG,' 'KLAS HORN' AND 'KLAS UGGLA' WERE SECURED ABREAST AT HARSF-JARDEN NAVAL BASE, WHEN AN EXPLOSION OCCURRED ABOARD 'GOTEBORG',...POSSIBLY A TORPEDO EXPLOSION. THE RESULTING FIRE AND FURTHER EXPLOSIONS SPREAD SO RAPIDLY THAT ALL THREE DESTROYERS SANK AT THEIR MOORINGS, THE FIRST TWO BROKEN IN HALF, AND THE OTHER ('KLAS UGGLA') WITH HER STERN BLOWN OFF. EVENTUALLY 'GOTEBORG' AND 'KLAS HORN' WERE SALVED AND REPAIRED...

DURING MANOEUVRES OFF PEARL HARBOR ON 29 MAY 1958, THE U.S. DESTROYER 'SILVERSTEIN' ACCIDENTLY RAMMED THE SUBMARINE 'STICKLEBACK'. THOUGH THE HALF-SUBMERGED SUBMARINE WAS ABLE TO SURFACE FOR HER CREW TO ESCAPE, SHE EVENTUALLY SANK TO THE BOTTOM...

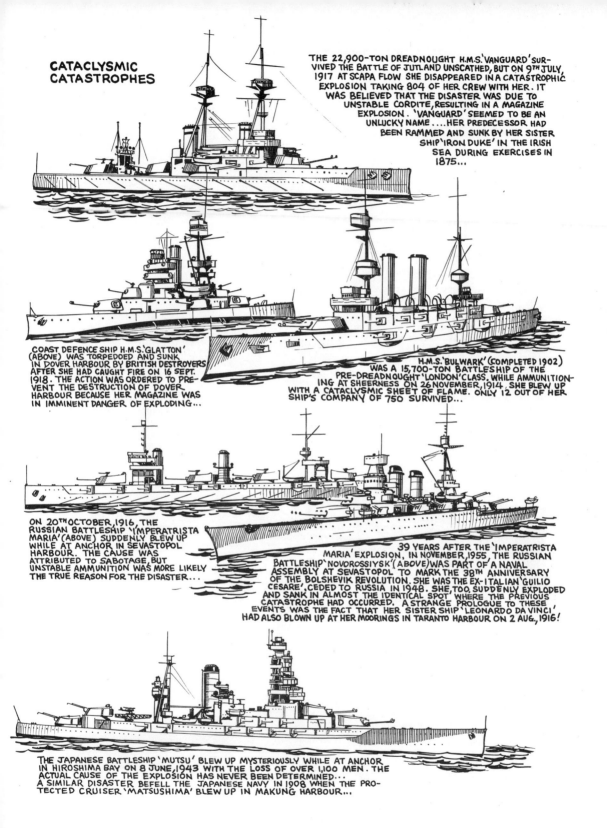

CATACLYSMIC CATASTROPHES

THE 22,900-TON DREADNOUGHT H.M.S. 'VANGUARD' SURVIVED THE BATTLE OF JUTLAND UNSCATHED, BUT ON 9TH JULY 1917 AT SCAPA FLOW SHE DISAPPEARED IN A CATASTROPHIC EXPLOSION TAKING 804 OF HER CREW WITH HER. IT WAS BELIEVED THAT THE DISASTER WAS DUE TO UNSTABLE CORDITE, RESULTING IN A MAGAZINE EXPLOSION. 'VANGUARD' SEEMED TO BE AN UNLUCKY NAME....HER PREDECESSOR HAD BEEN RAMMED AND SUNK BY HER SISTER SHIP 'IRON DUKE' IN THE IRISH SEA DURING EXERCISES IN 1875...

COAST DEFENCE SHIP H.M.S. 'GLATTON' (ABOVE) WAS TORPEDOED AND SUNK IN DOVER HARBOUR BY BRITISH DESTROYERS AFTER SHE HAD CAUGHT FIRE ON 16 SEPT. 1918. THE ACTION WAS ORDERED TO PREVENT THE DESTRUCTION OF DOVER HARBOUR BECAUSE HER MAGAZINE WAS IN IMMINENT DANGER OF EXPLODING...

H.M.S. 'BULWARK' (COMPLETED 1902) WAS A 15,700-TON BATTLESHIP OF THE PRE-DREADNOUGHT 'LONDON' CLASS. WHILE AMMUNITIONING AT SHEERNESS ON 26 NOVEMBER, 1914, SHE BLEW UP WITH A CATACLYSMIC SHEET OF FLAME. ONLY 12 OUT OF HER SHIP'S COMPANY OF 750 SURVIVED...

ON 20TH OCTOBER, 1916, THE RUSSIAN BATTLESHIP 'IMPERATRISTA MARIA' (ABOVE) SUDDENLY BLEW UP WHILE AT ANCHOR IN SEVASTOPOL HARBOUR. THE CAUSE WAS ATTRIBUTED TO SABOTAGE, BUT UNSTABLE AMMUNITION WAS MORE LIKELY THE TRUE REASON FOR THE DISASTER...

39 YEARS AFTER THE 'IMPERATRISTA MARIA' EXPLOSION, IN NOVEMBER, 1955, THE RUSSIAN BATTLESHIP 'NOVOROSSIYSK' (ABOVE) WAS PART OF A NAVAL ASSEMBLY AT SEVASTOPOL TO MARK THE 38TH ANNIVERSARY OF THE BOLSHEVIK REVOLUTION. SHE WAS THE EX-ITALIAN 'GUILIO CESARE', CEDED TO RUSSIA IN 1948. SHE, TOO, SUDDENLY EXPLODED AND SANK IN ALMOST THE IDENTICAL SPOT WHERE THE PREVIOUS CATASTROPHE HAD OCCURRED. A STRANGE PROLOGUE TO THESE EVENTS WAS THE FACT THAT HER SISTER SHIP 'LEONARDO DA VINCI' HAD ALSO BLOWN UP AT HER MOORINGS IN TARANTO HARBOUR ON 2 AUG, 1916!

THE JAPANESE BATTLESHIP 'MUTSU' BLEW UP MYSTERIOUSLY WHILE AT ANCHOR IN HIROSHIMA BAY ON 8 JUNE, 1943 WITH THE LOSS OF OVER 1,100 MEN. THE ACTUAL CAUSE OF THE EXPLOSION HAS NEVER BEEN DETERMINED... A SIMILAR DISASTER BEFELL THE JAPANESE NAVY IN 1908 WHEN THE PROTECTED CRUISER 'MATSUSHIMA' BLEW UP IN MAKUNG HARBOUR...

SHIPS THAT 'COMMITTED SUICIDE'...

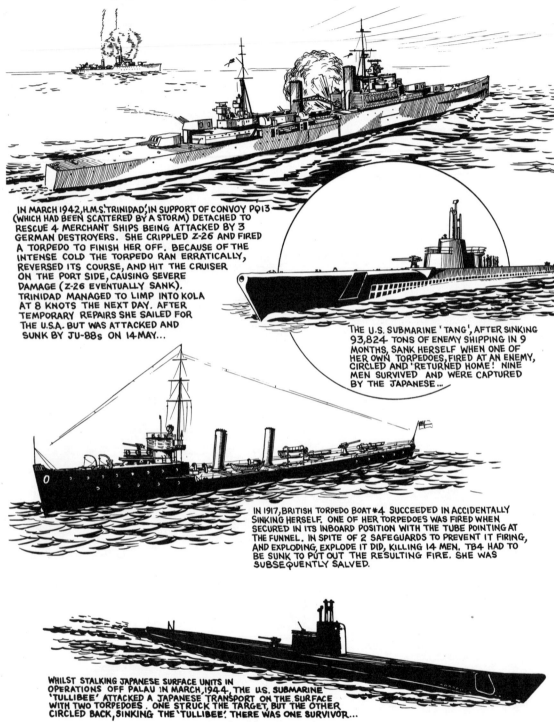

IN MARCH 1942, H.M.S. 'TRINIDAD', IN SUPPORT OF CONVOY PQ13 (WHICH HAD BEEN SCATTERED BY A STORM) DETACHED TO RESCUE 4 MERCHANT SHIPS BEING ATTACKED BY 3 GERMAN DESTROYERS. SHE CRIPPLED Z-26 AND FIRED A TORPEDO TO FINISH HER OFF. BECAUSE OF THE INTENSE COLD THE TORPEDO RAN ERRATICALLY, REVERSED ITS COURSE, AND HIT THE CRUISER ON THE PORT SIDE, CAUSING SEVERE DAMAGE (Z-26 EVENTUALLY SANK). TRINIDAD MANAGED TO LIMP INTO KOLA AT 8 KNOTS THE NEXT DAY. AFTER TEMPORARY REPAIRS SHE SAILED FOR THE U.S.A. BUT WAS ATTACKED AND SUNK BY JU-88s ON 14 MAY...

THE U.S. SUBMARINE 'TANG', AFTER SINKING 93,824 TONS OF ENEMY SHIPPING IN 9 MONTHS, SANK HERSELF WHEN ONE OF HER OWN TORPEDOES, FIRED AT AN ENEMY, CIRCLED AND 'RETURNED HOME'. NINE MEN SURVIVED AND WERE CAPTURED BY THE JAPANESE ...

IN 1917, BRITISH TORPEDO BOAT #4 SUCCEEDED IN ACCIDENTALLY SINKING HERSELF. ONE OF HER TORPEDOES WAS FIRED WHEN SECURED IN ITS INBOARD POSITION WITH THE TUBE POINTING AT THE FUNNEL. IN SPITE OF 2 SAFEGUARDS TO PREVENT IT FIRING, AND EXPLODING, EXPLODE IT DID, KILLING 14 MEN. TB4 HAD TO BE SUNK TO PUT OUT THE RESULTING FIRE. SHE WAS SUBSEQUENTLY SALVED.

WHILST STALKING JAPANESE SURFACE UNITS IN OPERATIONS OFF PALAU IN MARCH, 1944, THE U.S. SUBMARINE 'TULLIBEE' ATTACKED A JAPANESE TRANSPORT ON THE SURFACE WITH TWO TORPEDOES. ONE STRUCK THE TARGET, BUT THE OTHER CIRCLED BACK, SINKING THE 'TULLIBEE'. THERE WAS ONE SURVIVOR...

PART SIX

SECOND CAREERS

THE VAST majority of naval vessels end up at the breaker's yard after their service careers, but a few embark upon second careers after their original usefulness as fighting ships is over.

Naval vessels, because of their highly specialized nature, are normally very uneconomical propositions to convert to mercantile use. Few modern warships have been successfully rebuilt and employed profitably for any other job than that for which they were originally designed. There have, however, been some interesting exceptions.

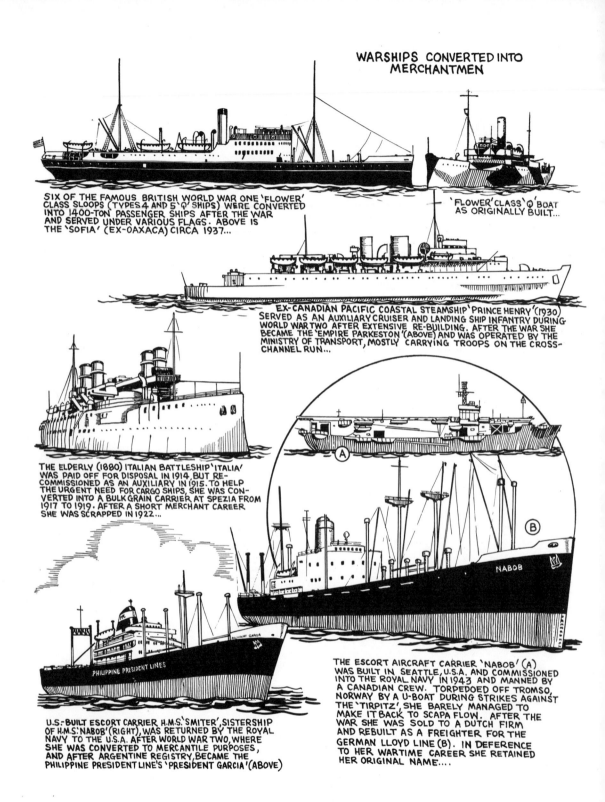

WARSHIPS CONVERTED INTO MERCHANTMEN

SIX OF THE FAMOUS BRITISH WORLD WAR ONE 'FLOWER' CLASS SLOOPS (TYPES 4 AND 5 'Q' SHIPS) WERE CONVERTED INTO 1400-TON PASSENGER SHIPS AFTER THE WAR AND SERVED UNDER VARIOUS FLAGS. ABOVE IS THE 'SOFIA' (EX-OAXACA) CIRCA 1937...

'FLOWER' CLASS 'Q' BOAT AS ORIGINALLY BUILT...

EX-CANADIAN PACIFIC COASTAL STEAMSHIP 'PRINCE HENRY' (1930) SERVED AS AN AUXILIARY CRUISER AND LANDING SHIP INFANTRY DURING WORLD WAR TWO AFTER EXTENSIVE RE-BUILDING. AFTER THE WAR SHE BECAME THE 'EMPIRE PARKESTON' (ABOVE) AND WAS OPERATED BY THE MINISTRY OF TRANSPORT, MOSTLY CARRYING TROOPS ON THE CROSS-CHANNEL RUN...

THE ELDERLY (1880) ITALIAN BATTLESHIP 'ITALIA' WAS PAID OFF FOR DISPOSAL IN 1914, BUT RE-COMMISSIONED AS AN AUXILIARY IN 1915. TO HELP THE URGENT NEED FOR CARGO SHIPS, SHE WAS CON-VERTED INTO A BULK GRAIN CARRIER AT SPEZIA FROM 1917 TO 1919. AFTER A SHORT MERCHANT CAREER SHE WAS SCRAPPED IN 1922...

THE ESCORT AIRCRAFT CARRIER 'NABOB' (A) WAS BUILT IN SEATTLE, U.S.A. AND COMMISSIONED INTO THE ROYAL NAVY IN 1943 AND MANNED BY A CANADIAN CREW. TORPEDOED OFF TROMSO, NORWAY BY A U-BOAT DURING STRIKES AGAINST THE 'TIRPITZ', SHE BARELY MANAGED TO MAKE IT BACK TO SCAPA FLOW. AFTER THE WAR SHE WAS SOLD TO A DUTCH FIRM AND REBUILT AS A FREIGHTER FOR THE GERMAN LLOYD LINE (B). IN DEFERENCE TO HER WARTIME CAREER SHE RETAINED HER ORIGINAL NAME....

U.S.-BUILT ESCORT CARRIER H.M.S. 'SMITER', SISTERSHIP OF H.M.S. 'NABOB' (RIGHT), WAS RETURNED BY THE ROYAL NAVY TO THE U.S.A. AFTER WORLD WAR TWO, WHERE SHE WAS CONVERTED TO MERCANTILE PURPOSES, AND AFTER ARGENTINE REGISTRY, BECAME THE PHILIPPINE PRESIDENT LINE'S 'PRESIDENT GARCIA' (ABOVE)

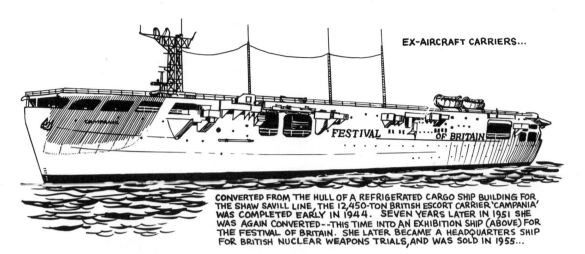

EX-AIRCRAFT CARRIERS...

FESTIVAL OF BRITAIN

CONVERTED FROM THE HULL OF A REFRIGERATED CARGO SHIP BUILDING FOR
THE SHAW SAVILL LINE, THE 12,450-TON BRITISH ESCORT CARRIER 'CAMPANIA'
WAS COMPLETED EARLY IN 1944. SEVEN YEARS LATER IN 1951 SHE
WAS AGAIN CONVERTED--THIS TIME INTO AN EXHIBITION SHIP (ABOVE) FOR
THE FESTIVAL OF BRITAIN. SHE LATER BECAME A HEADQUARTERS SHIP
FOR BRITISH NUCLEAR WEAPONS TRIALS, AND WAS SOLD IN 1955...

ONE OF THE FIRST ESCORT CARRIERS TO BE
COMPLETED, THE U.S.S.'LONG ISLAND' WAS
CONVERTED FROM AN INCOMPLETE MERCANTILE
HULL AT CHESTER, PENN. IN 1941. AFTER THE WAR
SHE BECAME THE EMMIGRANT AND
STUDENT CARRIER 'SEVEN SEAS'
(BELOW)...

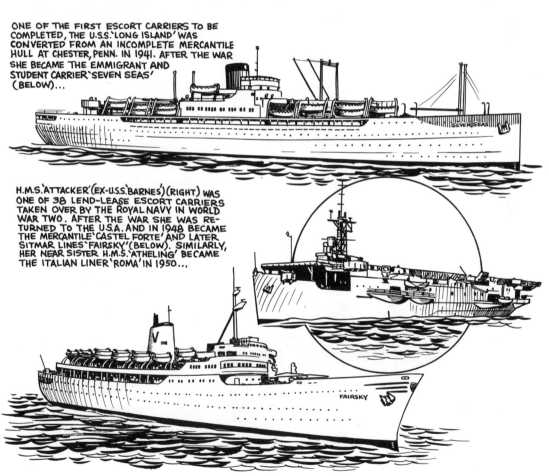

SEVEN SEAS

H.M.S.'ATTACKER'(EX-U.S.S.'BARNES')(RIGHT) WAS
ONE OF 38 LEND-LEASE ESCORT CARRIERS
TAKEN OVER BY THE ROYAL NAVY IN WORLD
WAR TWO. AFTER THE WAR SHE WAS RE-
TURNED TO THE U.S.A. AND IN 1948 BECAME
THE MERCANTILE'CASTEL FORTE' AND LATER
SITMAR LINES 'FAIRSKY'(BELOW). SIMILARLY,
HER NEAR SISTER H.M.S.'ATHELING' BECAME
THE ITALIAN LINER 'ROMA' IN 1950...

FAIRSKY

EX-WARSHIPS

A SUBSTANTIAL NUMBER OF MINOR WARSHIPS
FOUND CIVILIAN EMPLOYMENT AFTER THE WORLD
WARS AS PASSENGER SHIPS, COASTERS, YACHTS
AND TUGS, ETC. THE CONVERSIONS THAT THEY
UNDERWENT OFTEN OBLITERATED THEIR FORMER
LINES ALTOGETHER...

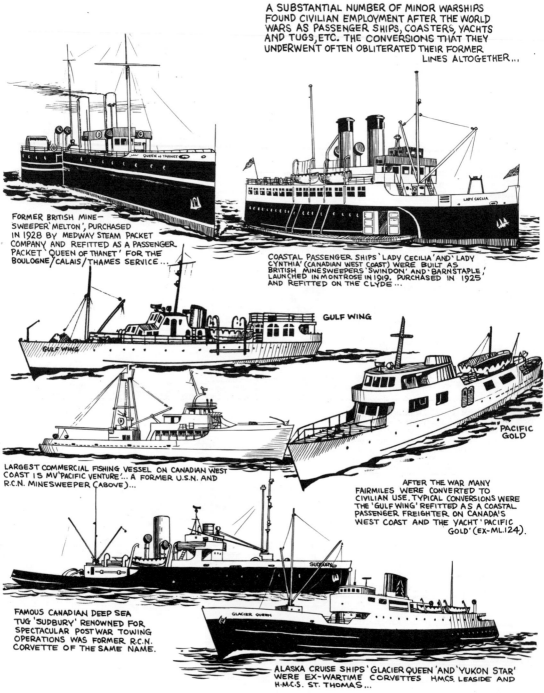

FORMER BRITISH MINE-
SWEEPER 'MELTON', PURCHASED
IN 1928 BY MEDWAY STEAM PACKET
COMPANY AND REFITTED AS A PASSENGER
PACKET 'QUEEN OF THANET' FOR THE
BOULOGNE/CALAIS/THAMES SERVICE...

COASTAL PASSENGER SHIPS 'LADY CECILIA' AND 'LADY
CYNTHIA' (CANADIAN WEST COAST) WERE BUILT AS
BRITISH MINESWEEPERS 'SWINDON' AND 'BARNSTAPLE',
LAUNCHED IN MONTROSE IN 1919. PURCHASED IN 1925
AND REFITTED ON THE CLYDE...

GULF WING

PACIFIC
GOLD

LARGEST COMMERCIAL FISHING VESSEL ON CANADIAN WEST
COAST IS MV 'PACIFIC VENTURE'... A FORMER U.S.N. AND
R.C.N. MINESWEEPER (ABOVE)...

AFTER THE WAR MANY
FAIRMILES WERE CONVERTED TO
CIVILIAN USE. TYPICAL CONVERSIONS WERE
THE 'GULF WING' REFITTED AS A COASTAL
PASSENGER FREIGHTER ON CANADA'S
WEST COAST AND THE YACHT 'PACIFIC
GOLD' (EX-ML.124).

FAMOUS CANADIAN DEEP SEA
TUG 'SUDBURY' RENOWNED FOR
SPECTACULAR POSTWAR TOWING
OPERATIONS WAS FORMER R.C.N.
CORVETTE OF THE SAME NAME.

ALASKA CRUISE SHIPS 'GLACIER QUEEN' AND 'YUKON STAR'
WERE EX-WARTIME CORVETTES HMCS. LEASIDE AND
H.M.C.S. ST. THOMAS...

EX-WARRIORS...

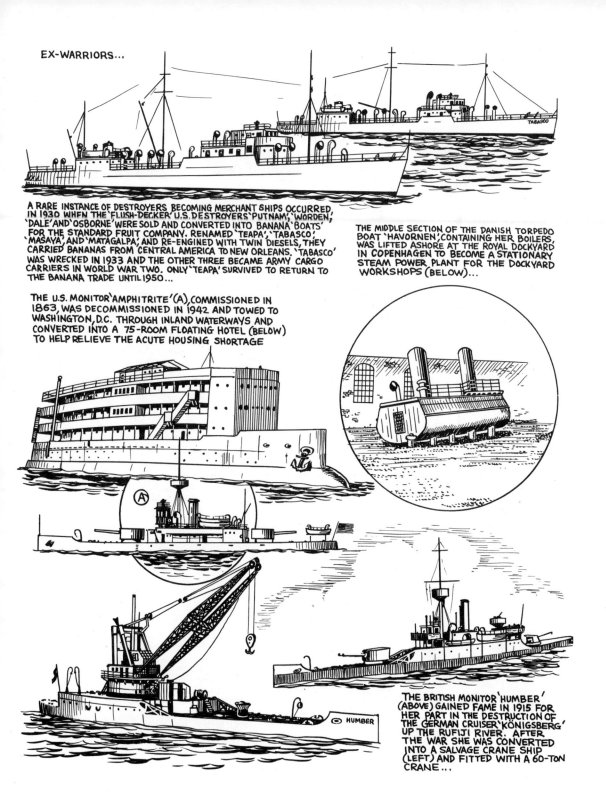

A RARE INSTANCE OF DESTROYERS BECOMING MERCHANT SHIPS OCCURRED IN 1930 WHEN THE 'FLUSH-DECKER' U.S. DESTROYERS 'PUTNAM', 'WORDEN', 'DALE' AND 'OSBORNE' WERE SOLD AND CONVERTED INTO BANANA 'BOATS' FOR THE STANDARD FRUIT COMPANY. RENAMED 'TEAPA', 'TABASCO', 'MASAYA', AND 'MATAGALPA', AND RE-ENGINED WITH TWIN DIESELS, THEY CARRIED BANANAS FROM CENTRAL AMERICA TO NEW ORLEANS. 'TABASCO' WAS WRECKED IN 1933 AND THE OTHER THREE BECAME ARMY CARGO CARRIERS IN WORLD WAR TWO. ONLY 'TEAPA' SURVIVED TO RETURN TO THE BANANA TRADE UNTIL 1950...

THE MIDDLE SECTION OF THE DANISH TORPEDO BOAT 'HAVORNEN', CONTAINING HER BOILERS, WAS LIFTED ASHORE AT THE ROYAL DOCKYARD IN COPENHAGEN TO BECOME A STATIONARY STEAM POWER PLANT FOR THE DOCKYARD WORKSHOPS (BELOW)...

THE U.S. MONITOR 'AMPHITRITE' (A), COMMISSIONED IN 1863, WAS DECOMMISSIONED IN 1942 AND TOWED TO WASHINGTON, D.C. THROUGH INLAND WATERWAYS AND CONVERTED INTO A 75-ROOM FLOATING HOTEL (BELOW) TO HELP RELIEVE THE ACUTE HOUSING SHORTAGE

THE BRITISH MONITOR 'HUMBER' (ABOVE) GAINED FAME IN 1915 FOR HER PART IN THE DESTRUCTION OF THE GERMAN CRUISER 'KÖNIGSBERG' UP THE RUFIJI RIVER. AFTER THE WAR SHE WAS CONVERTED INTO A SALVAGE CRANE SHIP (LEFT) AND FITTED WITH A 60-TON CRANE...

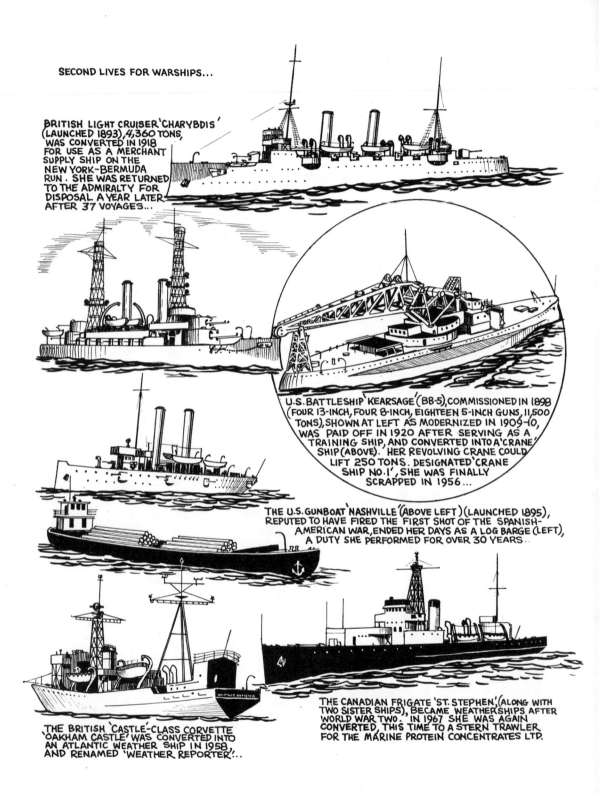

SECOND LIVES FOR WARSHIPS...

BRITISH LIGHT CRUISER 'CHARYBDIS' (LAUNCHED 1893), 4,360 TONS, WAS CONVERTED IN 1918 FOR USE AS A MERCHANT SUPPLY SHIP ON THE NEW YORK-BERMUDA RUN. SHE WAS RETURNED TO THE ADMIRALTY FOR DISPOSAL A YEAR LATER, AFTER 37 VOYAGES...

U.S. BATTLESHIP 'KEARSAGE' (BB-5), COMMISSIONED IN 1898 (FOUR 13-INCH, FOUR 8-INCH, EIGHTEEN 5-INCH GUNS, 11,500 TONS), SHOWN AT LEFT AS MODERNIZED IN 1909-10, WAS PAID OFF IN 1920 AFTER SERVING AS A TRAINING SHIP, AND CONVERTED INTO A 'CRANE' SHIP (ABOVE). HER REVOLVING CRANE COULD LIFT 250 TONS. DESIGNATED 'CRANE SHIP NO.1', SHE WAS FINALLY SCRAPPED IN 1956...

THE U.S. GUNBOAT 'NASHVILLE' (ABOVE LEFT) (LAUNCHED 1895), REPUTED TO HAVE FIRED THE FIRST SHOT OF THE SPANISH-AMERICAN WAR, ENDED HER DAYS AS A LOG BARGE (LEFT), A DUTY SHE PERFORMED FOR OVER 30 YEARS...

THE BRITISH 'CASTLE'-CLASS CORVETTE 'OAKHAM CASTLE' WAS CONVERTED INTO AN ATLANTIC WEATHER SHIP IN 1958 AND RENAMED 'WEATHER REPORTER'...

THE CANADIAN FRIGATE 'ST. STEPHEN' (ALONG WITH TWO SISTER SHIPS), BECAME WEATHERSHIPS AFTER WORLD WAR TWO. IN 1967 SHE WAS AGAIN CONVERTED, THIS TIME TO A STERN TRAWLER FOR THE MARINE PROTEIN CONCENTRATES LTD.

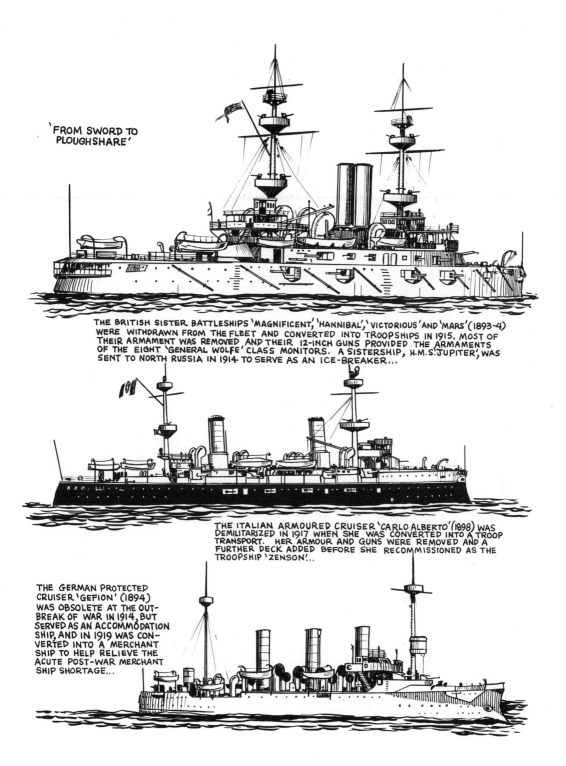

'FROM SWORD TO PLOUGHSHARE'

THE BRITISH SISTER BATTLESHIPS 'MAGNIFICENT', 'HANNIBAL', 'VICTORIOUS' AND 'MARS' (1893-4) WERE WITHDRAWN FROM THE FLEET AND CONVERTED INTO TROOPSHIPS IN 1915. MOST OF THEIR ARMAMENT WAS REMOVED AND THEIR 12-INCH GUNS PROVIDED THE ARMAMENTS OF THE EIGHT 'GENERAL WOLFE' CLASS MONITORS. A SISTERSHIP, H.M.S. 'JUPITER', WAS SENT TO NORTH RUSSIA IN 1914 TO SERVE AS AN ICE-BREAKER...

THE ITALIAN ARMOURED CRUISER 'CARLO ALBERTO' (1898) WAS DEMILITARIZED IN 1917 WHEN SHE WAS CONVERTED INTO A TROOP TRANSPORT. HER ARMOUR AND GUNS WERE REMOVED AND A FURTHER DECK ADDED BEFORE SHE RECOMMISSIONED AS THE TROOPSHIP 'ZENSON'...

THE GERMAN PROTECTED CRUISER 'GEFION' (1894) WAS OBSOLETE AT THE OUTBREAK OF WAR IN 1914, BUT SERVED AS AN ACCOMMODATION SHIP, AND IN 1919 WAS CONVERTED INTO A MERCHANT SHIP TO HELP RELIEVE THE ACUTE POST-WAR MERCHANT SHIP SHORTAGE...

'DOUBLE LIVES'

ATTEMPTS HAVE BEEN MADE ...NOT ALWAYS SUCCESSFULLY...TO CONVERT WARSHIPS INTO MERCHANT VESSELS, OR TO USE THEM FOR PURPOSES OTHER THAN FOR WHICH THEY WERE DESIGNED. HERE ARE A FEW VARIED EXAMPLES,

THE FRENCH CRUISER 'DUPUY de LÔME'(1890), THE FINEST CRUISER OF HER DAY, WAS SOLD TO PERU IN 1914, BUT REMAINED IN THE FRENCH SERVICE DURING THE WAR. IN 1919 SHE WAS BOUGHT BY A BELGIAN CONCERN, REMODELLED INTO A CARGO STEAMER, AND RENAMED 'PERUVIER.' 12 OF HER 18 BOILERS AND 2 OF HER SCREWS WERE REMOVED. SHE LEFT CARDIFF FOR RIO WITH A CARGO OF COAL, BROKE DOWN, CAUGHT FIRE AND WAS TOWED TO PERNAMBUCO, AND THEN BACK TO ANTWERP WHERE SHE WAS SCRAPPED!

(BELOW) IN 1935 TWO EX-ROYAL NAVY SUBMARINES WERE USED AS SALVAGE PONTOONS TO RAISE THE SEMI-SUBMERGED STEAMER 'ERROL' WHICH WAS LYING IN THE FIRTH OF FORTH. SHE WAS BROUGHT TO THE SURFACE BY BLOWING THE SUBMARINES' BALLAST TANKS...

THE BRITISH WORLD WAR ONE MINESWEEPER 'FORD' BECAME A CAR FERRY AFTER THE WAR ON THE DOVER-CALAIS RUN. SHE LOADED AND CARRIED THE CARS ON DECK. THE SLOOP H.M.S.'PEONY' ALSO SERVED THE SOUTHERN RAILWAY ON THE CROSS-CHANNEL SERVICE. SIMILAR CONVERSIONS WERE MADE AFTER WORLD WAR TWO WITH A FRIGATE AND SEVERAL L.S.T.s...

AS A DESPERATE MEASURE TO SUPPLY HER TROOPS IN AFRICA IN 1942, ITALY USED SEVERAL OCEAN-GOING 'BALILLA' CLASS SUBMARINES AS TANKERS. STRIPPED TO THE BARE HULL AND WITH ENGINES REMOVED, THEY WERE TOWED SEMI-SUBMERGED BY DESTROYERS AT HIGH SPEED TO BENGAZI AND TOBRUK ...

'CIVILIZED INVADERS'
(EX-LANDING CRAFT)

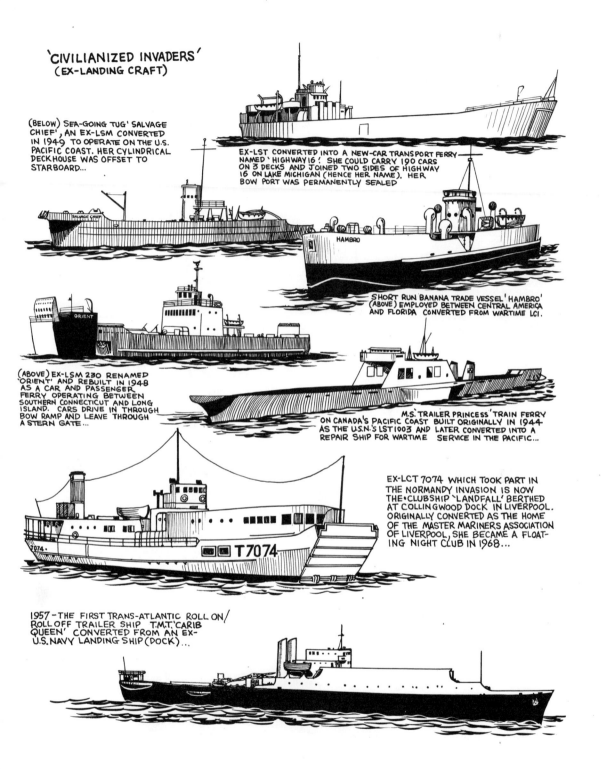

(BELOW) SEA-GOING TUG 'SALVAGE CHIEF', AN EX-LSM CONVERTED IN 1949 TO OPERATE ON THE U.S. PACIFIC COAST. HER CYLINDRICAL DECKHOUSE WAS OFFSET TO STARBOARD...

EX-LST CONVERTED INTO A NEW-CAR TRANSPORT FERRY NAMED 'HIGHWAY 16'. SHE COULD CARRY 190 CARS ON 3 DECKS AND JOINED TWO SIDES OF HIGHWAY 16 ON LAKE MICHIGAN (HENCE HER NAME). HER BOW PORT WAS PERMANENTLY SEALED.

SHORT RUN BANANA TRADE VESSEL 'HAMBRO' (ABOVE) EMPLOYED BETWEEN CENTRAL AMERICA AND FLORIDA CONVERTED FROM WARTIME LCI.

(ABOVE) EX-LSM 230 RENAMED 'ORIENT' AND REBUILT IN 1948 AS A CAR AND PASSENGER FERRY OPERATING BETWEEN SOUTHERN CONNECTICUT AND LONG ISLAND. CARS DRIVE IN THROUGH BOW RAMP AND LEAVE THROUGH A STERN GATE...

M.S. 'TRAILER PRINCESS' TRAIN FERRY ON CANADA'S PACIFIC COAST BUILT ORIGINALLY IN 1944 AS THE U.S.N.'S LST 1003 AND LATER CONVERTED INTO A REPAIR SHIP FOR WARTIME SERVICE IN THE PACIFIC...

EX-LCT 7074 WHICH TOOK PART IN THE NORMANDY INVASION IS NOW THE 'CLUBSHIP 'LANDFALL' BERTHED AT COLLINGWOOD DOCK IN LIVERPOOL. ORIGINALLY CONVERTED AS THE HOME OF THE MASTER MARINERS ASSOCIATION OF LIVERPOOL, SHE BECAME A FLOATING NIGHT CLUB IN 1968...

1957 – THE FIRST TRANS-ATLANTIC ROLL ON/ ROLL OFF TRAILER SHIP T.M.T. 'CARIB QUEEN' CONVERTED FROM AN EX- U.S. NAVY LANDING SHIP (DOCK)...

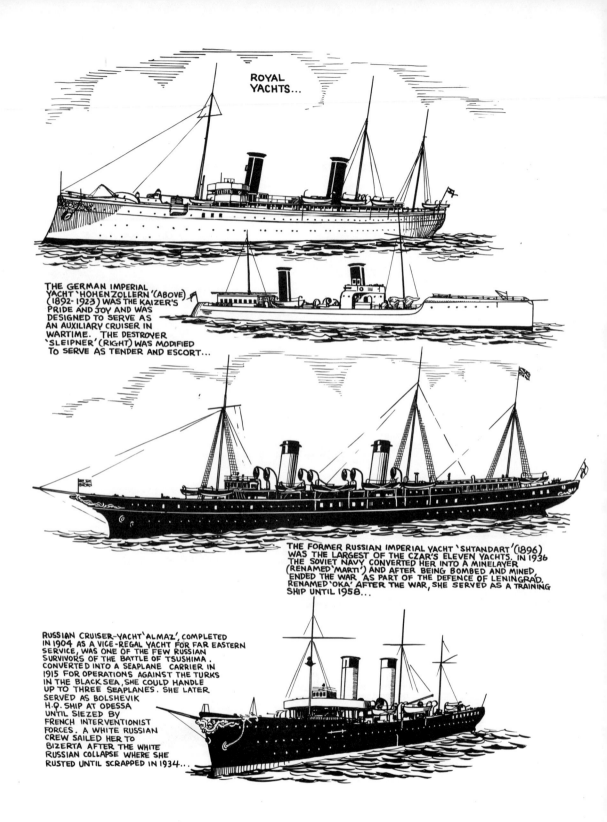

ROYAL
YACHTS...

THE GERMAN IMPERIAL
YACHT 'HOHENZOLLERN' (ABOVE)
(1892-1923) WAS THE KAIZER'S
PRIDE AND JOY AND WAS
DESIGNED TO SERVE AS
AN AUXILIARY CRUISER IN
WARTIME. THE DESTROYER
'SLEIPNER' (RIGHT) WAS MODIFIED
TO SERVE AS TENDER AND ESCORT...

THE FORMER RUSSIAN IMPERIAL YACHT 'SHTANDART' (1896)
WAS THE LARGEST OF THE CZAR'S ELEVEN YACHTS. IN 1936
THE SOVIET NAVY CONVERTED HER INTO A MINELAYER
(RENAMED 'MARTI') AND AFTER BEING BOMBED AND MINED
ENDED THE WAR AS PART OF THE DEFENCE OF LENINGRAD.
RENAMED 'OKA' AFTER THE WAR, SHE SERVED AS A TRAINING
SHIP UNTIL 1958...

RUSSIAN CRUISER-YACHT 'ALMAZ', COMPLETED
IN 1904 AS A VICE-REGAL YACHT FOR FAR EASTERN
SERVICE, WAS ONE OF THE FEW RUSSIAN
SURVIVORS OF THE BATTLE OF TSUSHIMA.
CONVERTED INTO A SEAPLANE CARRIER IN
1915 FOR OPERATIONS AGAINST THE TURKS
IN THE BLACK SEA, SHE COULD HANDLE
UP TO THREE SEAPLANES. SHE LATER
SERVED AS BOLSHEVIK
H.Q. SHIP AT ODESSA
UNTIL SIEZED BY
FRENCH INTERVENTIONIST
FORCES. A WHITE RUSSIAN
CREW SAILED HER TO
BIZERTA AFTER THE WHITE
RUSSIAN COLLAPSE WHERE SHE
RUSTED UNTIL SCRAPPED IN 1934...

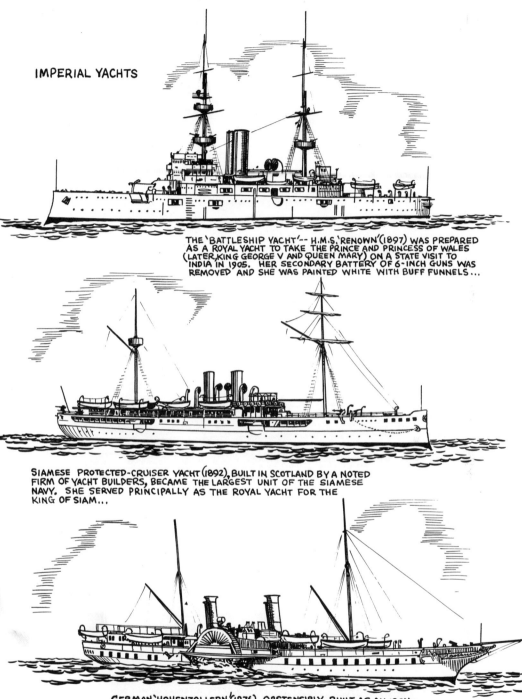

IMPERIAL YACHTS

THE 'BATTLESHIP YACHT'-- H.M.S.'RENOWN'(1897) WAS PREPARED
AS A ROYAL YACHT TO TAKE THE PRINCE AND PRINCESS OF WALES
(LATER,KING GEORGE V AND QUEEN MARY) ON A STATE VISIT TO
INDIA IN 1905. HER SECONDARY BATTERY OF 6-INCH GUNS WAS
REMOVED AND SHE WAS PAINTED WHITE WITH BUFF FUNNELS...

SIAMESE PROTECTED-CRUISER YACHT (1892), BUILT IN SCOTLAND BY A NOTED
FIRM OF YACHT BUILDERS, BECAME THE LARGEST UNIT OF THE SIAMESE
NAVY. SHE SERVED PRINCIPALLY AS THE ROYAL YACHT FOR THE
KING OF SIAM...

GERMAN 'HOHENZOLLERN' (1876), OBSTENSIBLY BUILT AS AN IRON-
HULLED PADDLE-WHEEL DESPATCH VESSEL, BUT OFFICIALLY RATED
AS 'ROYAL YACHT' IN 1880. IN 1892 SHE WAS REPLACED BY THE
NEW AND LARGER 'HOHENZOLLERN', AND RENAMED 'KAISERADLER'...

YACHTS AT WAR...

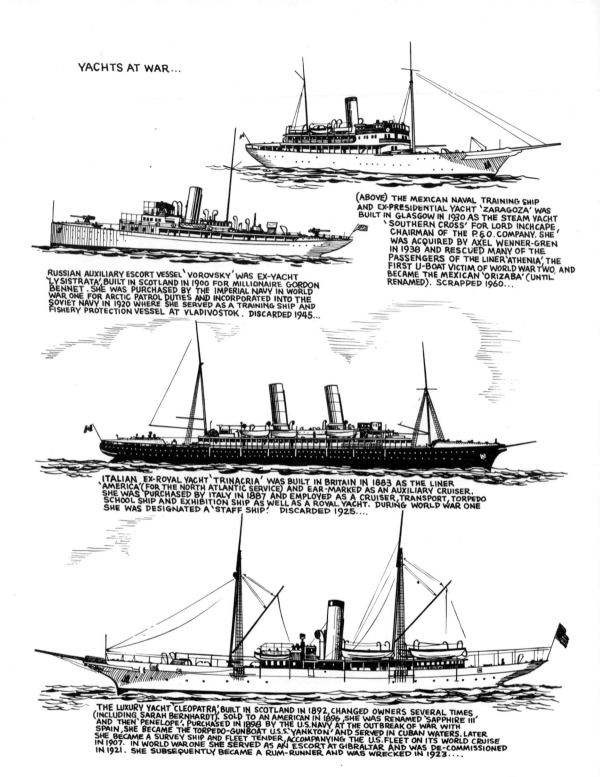

(ABOVE) THE MEXICAN NAVAL TRAINING SHIP AND EX-PRESIDENTIAL YACHT 'ZARAGOZA' WAS BUILT IN GLASGOW IN 1930 AS THE STEAM YACHT 'SOUTHERN CROSS' FOR LORD INCHCAPE, CHAIRMAN OF THE P.&O. COMPANY. SHE WAS ACQUIRED BY AXEL WENNER-GREN IN 1938 AND RESCUED MANY OF THE PASSENGERS OF THE LINER 'ATHENIA', THE FIRST U-BOAT VICTIM OF WORLD WAR TWO, AND BECAME THE MEXICAN 'ORIZABA' (UNTIL RENAMED). SCRAPPED 1960...

RUSSIAN AUXILIARY ESCORT VESSEL 'VOROVSKY' WAS EX-YACHT 'LYSISTRATA', BUILT IN SCOTLAND IN 1900 FOR MILLIONAIRE GORDON BENNET. SHE WAS PURCHASED BY THE IMPERIAL NAVY IN WORLD WAR ONE FOR ARCTIC PATROL DUTIES AND INCORPORATED INTO THE SOVIET NAVY IN 1920 WHERE SHE SERVED AS A TRAINING SHIP AND FISHERY PROTECTION VESSEL AT VLADIVOSTOK. DISCARDED 1945...

ITALIAN EX-ROYAL YACHT 'TRINACRIA' WAS BUILT IN BRITAIN IN 1883 AS THE LINER 'AMERICA' (FOR THE NORTH ATLANTIC SERVICE) AND EAR-MARKED AS AN AUXILIARY CRUISER. SHE WAS PURCHASED BY ITALY IN 1887 AND EMPLOYED AS A CRUISER, TRANSPORT, TORPEDO SCHOOL SHIP AND EXHIBITION SHIP AS WELL AS A ROYAL YACHT. DURING WORLD WAR ONE SHE WAS DESIGNATED A 'STAFF SHIP'. DISCARDED 1925....

THE LUXURY YACHT 'CLEOPATRA' BUILT IN SCOTLAND IN 1892, CHANGED OWNERS SEVERAL TIMES (INCLUDING SARAH BERNHARDT). SOLD TO AN AMERICAN IN 1896 SHE WAS RENAMED 'SAPPHIRE III' AND THEN 'PENELOPE'. PURCHASED IN 1898 BY THE U.S.NAVY AT THE OUTBREAK OF WAR WITH SPAIN, SHE BECAME THE TORPEDO-GUNBOAT U.S.S.'YANKTON' AND SERVED IN CUBAN WATERS. LATER SHE BECAME A SURVEY SHIP AND FLEET TENDER, ACCOMPANYING THE U.S.FLEET ON ITS WORLD CRUISE IN 1907. IN WORLD WAR ONE SHE SERVED AS AN ESCORT AT GIBRALTAR AND WAS DE-COMMISSIONED IN 1921. SHE SUBSEQUENTLY BECAME A RUM-RUNNER AND WAS WRECKED IN 1923....

YACHTS IN GREY

THE U.S. FINANCIER J.P. MORGAN AND HIS SON OWNED FOUR STEAM YACHTS, ALL NAMED 'CORSAIR', TWO OF WHICH SERVED IN THE U.S. NAVY, AND ONE IN THE ROYAL NAVY. THE SECOND 'CORSAIR' (BUILT 1889) BECAME THE DISPATCH VESSEL 'U.S.S. GLOUCESTER' IN 1898 (SPANISH-AMERICAN WAR). THE THIRD 'CORSAIR' (1898/9) BECAME A CONVOY ESCORT FROM 1917 TO 1919, ARMED WITH FOUR 3-INCH GUNS. IN 1930 SHE BECAME THE U.S. COAST AND GEODETIC SURVEY SHIP 'OCEANOGRAPHER' AND SERVED IN THE U.S. NAVY AGAIN FROM 1942 TO 1944 (SEE ABOVE). THE FOURTH AND LARGEST 'CORSAIR' (1930, 2,142 TONS), JOINED THE ROYAL NAVY IN 1940 AND BECAME A FLEET AIR ARM TARGET VESSEL AT BERMUDA. AFTER THE WAR SHE BECAME A CRUISE SHIP, BUT WAS WRECKED IN 1949...

THE WORLD WAR TWO U.S. COASTAL PATROL VESSEL 'U.S.S. AMBER' (ABOVE) WAS FORMERLY ACTOR JOHN BARRYMORE'S LUXURY YACHT 'INFANTA' BUILT IN 1930. AFTER THE WAR SHE WAS RENAMED 'POLARIS' AND BECAME AN OIL RESEARCH VESSEL IN THE PACIFIC. IN 1946 SHE WAS PURCHASED BY THE 'FOSS LAUNCH AND TUG CO.' OF PUGET SOUND, AND RE-NAMED 'THEA FOSS'...

THE STEAM YACHT 'MEDEA', BUILT IN SCOTLAND IN 1904 FOR A WEALTHY LAIRD, SERVED IN TWO WARS AND THREE NAVIES. IN WORLD WAR ONE SHE BECAME A FRENCH PATROL CRAFT, ARMED WITH A 75-MM GUN, DEPTH CHARGES, AND AN OBSERVATION BALLOON. IN WORLD WAR TWO, THE ROYAL NAVY EMPLOYED HER AS A BARRAGE BALLOON TENDER, AND SHE LATER BECAME A SUBMARINE SUPPLY AND ACCOMMODATION SHIP FOR THE FREE NORWEGIAN NAVY. SHE IS NOW ON DISPLAY AT THE SAN DIEGO MARITIME MUSEUM...

'U.S.S. EAGLE' (434 TONS) (ABOVE), WAS BUILT IN 1890 AS A LUXURY STEAM YACHT. TAKEN OVER BY THE U.S. NAVY BEFORE WORLD WAR ONE, SHE WAS CONVERTED INTO A SURVEY SHIP AND ARMED WITH TWO 6-POUNDERS. IN 1917 HER INTERVENTION IN REVOLUTIONARY-TORN CUBA HELPED TO PREVENT SEVERAL SERIOUS INCIDENTS...

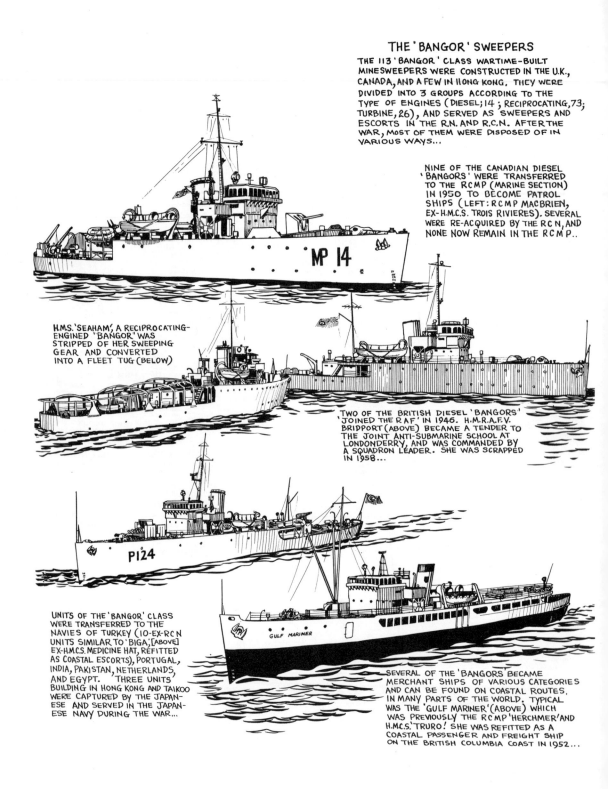

THE 'BANGOR' SWEEPERS

THE 113 'BANGOR' CLASS WARTIME-BUILT MINESWEEPERS WERE CONSTRUCTED IN THE U.K., CANADA, AND A FEW IN HONG KONG. THEY WERE DIVIDED INTO 3 GROUPS ACCORDING TO THE TYPE OF ENGINES (DIESEL; 14; RECIPROCATING, 73; TURBINE, 26), AND SERVED AS SWEEPERS AND ESCORTS IN THE R.N. AND R.C.N. AFTER THE WAR, MOST OF THEM WERE DISPOSED OF IN VARIOUS WAYS...

NINE OF THE CANADIAN DIESEL 'BANGORS' WERE TRANSFERRED TO THE RCMP (MARINE SECTION) IN 1950 TO BECOME PATROL SHIPS (LEFT: RCMP MACBRIEN, EX-H.M.C.S. TROIS RIVIERES). SEVERAL WERE RE-ACQUIRED BY THE RCN, AND NONE NOW REMAIN IN THE RCMP..

MP 14

H.M.S. 'SEAHAM', A RECIPROCATING-ENGINED 'BANGOR' WAS STRIPPED OF HER SWEEPING GEAR AND CONVERTED INTO A FLEET TUG (BELOW)

TWO OF THE BRITISH DIESEL 'BANGORS' JOINED THE RAF IN 1946. H.M.R.A.F.V. BRIDPORT (ABOVE) BECAME A TENDER TO THE JOINT ANTI-SUBMARINE SCHOOL AT LONDONDERRY, AND WAS COMMANDED BY A SQUADRON LEADER. SHE WAS SCRAPPED IN 1958...

P124

UNITS OF THE 'BANGOR' CLASS WERE TRANSFERRED TO THE NAVIES OF TURKEY (10-EX-RCN UNITS SIMILAR TO 'BIGA', [ABOVE] EX-H.M.C.S. MEDICINE HAT, REFITTED AS COASTAL ESCORTS), PORTUGAL, INDIA, PAKISTAN, NETHERLANDS, AND EGYPT. THREE UNITS BUILDING IN HONG KONG AND TAIKOO WERE CAPTURED BY THE JAPANESE AND SERVED IN THE JAPANESE NAVY DURING THE WAR...

GULF MARINER

SEVERAL OF THE 'BANGORS' BECAME MERCHANT SHIPS OF VARIOUS CATEGORIES AND CAN BE FOUND ON COASTAL ROUTES, IN MANY PARTS OF THE WORLD. TYPICAL WAS THE 'GULF MARINER' (ABOVE) WHICH WAS PREVIOUSLY THE RCMP 'HERCHMER' AND H.M.C.S. 'TRURO'. SHE WAS REFITTED AS A COASTAL PASSENGER AND FREIGHT SHIP ON THE BRITISH COLUMBIA COAST IN 1952...

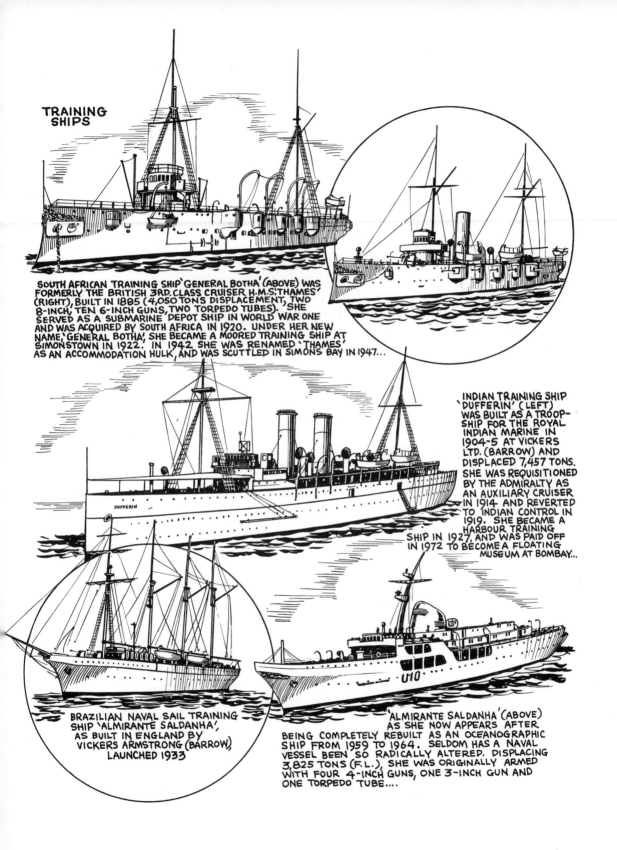

TRAINING SHIPS

SOUTH AFRICAN TRAINING SHIP 'GENERAL BOTHA' (ABOVE) WAS FORMERLY THE BRITISH 3RD. CLASS CRUISER H.M.S. 'THAMES' (RIGHT), BUILT IN 1885 (4,050 TONS DISPLACEMENT, TWO 8-INCH, TEN 6-INCH GUNS, TWO TORPEDO TUBES). SHE SERVED AS A SUBMARINE DEPOT SHIP IN WORLD WAR ONE AND WAS ACQUIRED BY SOUTH AFRICA IN 1920. UNDER HER NEW NAME, 'GENERAL BOTHA', SHE BECAME A MOORED TRAINING SHIP AT SIMONSTOWN IN 1922. IN 1942 SHE WAS RENAMED 'THAMES' AS AN ACCOMMODATION HULK, AND WAS SCUTTLED IN SIMONS BAY IN 1947...

INDIAN TRAINING SHIP 'DUFFERIN' (LEFT) WAS BUILT AS A TROOP-SHIP FOR THE ROYAL INDIAN MARINE IN 1904-5 AT VICKERS LTD. (BARROW) AND DISPLACED 7,457 TONS. SHE WAS REQUISITIONED BY THE ADMIRALTY AS AN AUXILIARY CRUISER IN 1914 AND REVERTED TO INDIAN CONTROL IN 1919. SHE BECAME A HARBOUR TRAINING SHIP IN 1927, AND WAS PAID OFF IN 1972 TO BECOME A FLOATING MUSEUM AT BOMBAY...

BRAZILIAN NAVAL SAIL TRAINING SHIP 'ALMIRANTE SALDANHA', AS BUILT IN ENGLAND BY VICKERS ARMSTRONG (BARROW) LAUNCHED 1933

'ALMIRANTE SALDANHA' (ABOVE) AS SHE NOW APPEARS AFTER BEING COMPLETELY REBUILT AS AN OCEANOGRAPHIC SHIP FROM 1959 TO 1964. SELDOM HAS A NAVAL VESSEL BEEN SO RADICALLY ALTERED. DISPLACING 3,825 TONS (F.L.), SHE WAS ORIGINALLY ARMED WITH FOUR 4-INCH GUNS, ONE 3-INCH GUN AND ONE TORPEDO TUBE....

PART SEVEN

NAVAL VIGNETTES

NOT INAPPROPRIATE in a compendium of naval matters is a collection of vignettes that, because of their diversity, cannot be categorized under a single heading. These include recollections of twentieth century naval mutinies, extraordinary single-ship actions, warships that served under two or more ensigns as a result of capture or capitulation, and unique squadrons which played a part in formulating the naval history of two world wars. Any such collection of anecdotes can never hope to accomplish more than merely to scratch the surface of these numerous and interesting subjects.

MODERN MUTINIES...

THE 20TH CENTURY IS NO EXCEPTION WHEN IT COMES TO SAILORS UPRISINGS AGAINST THEIR OFFICERS AND/OR REGIMES... FROM FLEET-WIDE MUTINIES SUCH AS IN GERMANY IN 1917 AND 1918, TO SINGLE-SHIP EPISODES THAT ACHIEVED MUCH NOTORIETY AND BLOODSHED...

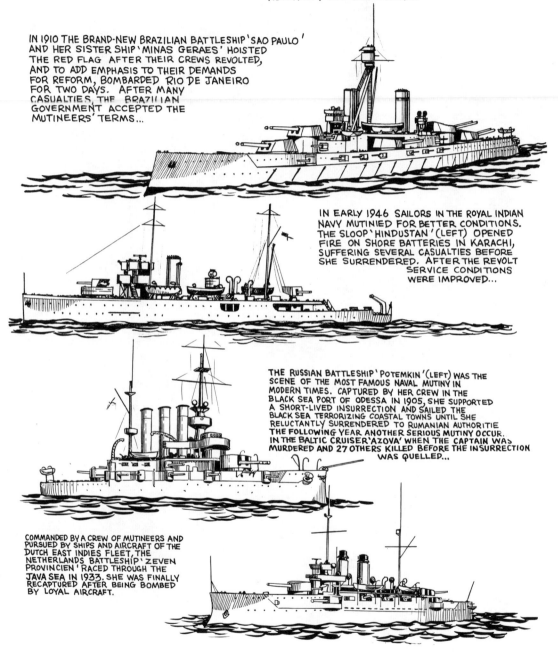

IN 1910 THE BRAND-NEW BRAZILIAN BATTLESHIP 'SAO PAULO' AND HER SISTER SHIP 'MINAS GERAES' HOISTED THE RED FLAG AFTER THEIR CREWS REVOLTED, AND TO ADD EMPHASIS TO THEIR DEMANDS FOR REFORM, BOMBARDED RIO DE JANEIRO FOR TWO DAYS. AFTER MANY CASUALTIES, THE BRAZILIAN GOVERNMENT ACCEPTED THE MUTINEERS' TERMS...

IN EARLY 1946 SAILORS IN THE ROYAL INDIAN NAVY MUTINIED FOR BETTER CONDITIONS. THE SLOOP 'HINDUSTAN' (LEFT) OPENED FIRE ON SHORE BATTERIES IN KARACHI, SUFFERING SEVERAL CASUALTIES BEFORE SHE SURRENDERED. AFTER THE REVOLT SERVICE CONDITIONS WERE IMPROVED...

THE RUSSIAN BATTLESHIP 'POTEMKIN' (LEFT) WAS THE SCENE OF THE MOST FAMOUS NAVAL MUTINY IN MODERN TIMES. CAPTURED BY HER CREW IN THE BLACK SEA PORT OF ODESSA IN 1905, SHE SUPPORTED A SHORT-LIVED INSURRECTION AND SAILED THE BLACK SEA TERRORIZING COASTAL TOWNS UNTIL SHE RELUCTANTLY SURRENDERED TO RUMANIAN AUTHORITIE THE FOLLOWING YEAR ANOTHER SERIOUS MUTINY OCCUR. IN THE BALTIC CRUISER 'AZOVA' WHEN THE CAPTAIN WAS MURDERED AND 27 OTHERS KILLED BEFORE THE INSURRECTION WAS QUELLED...

COMMANDED BY A CREW OF MUTINEERS AND PURSUED BY SHIPS AND AIRCRAFT OF THE DUTCH EAST INDIES FLEET, THE NETHERLANDS BATTLESHIP 'ZEVEN PROVINCIEN' RACED THROUGH THE JAVA SEA IN 1933. SHE WAS FINALLY RECAPTURED AFTER BEING BOMBED BY LOYAL AIRCRAFT.

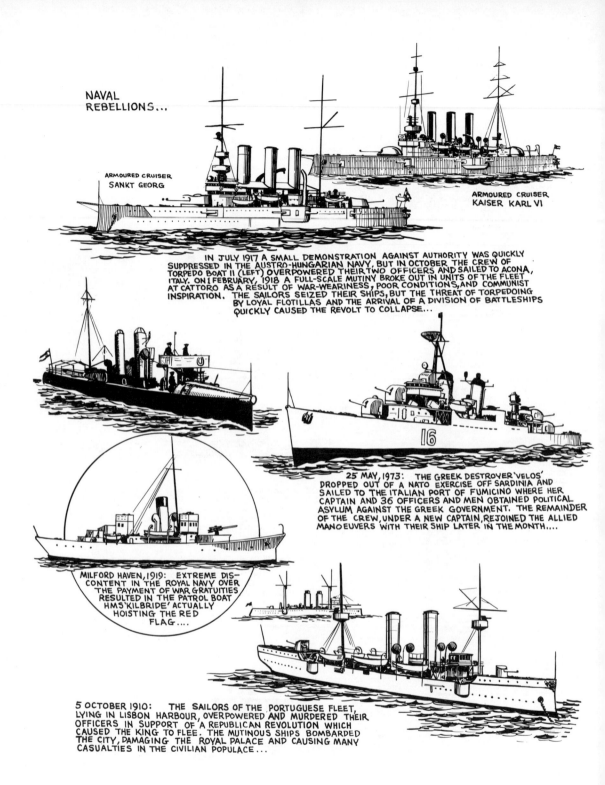

NAVAL REBELLIONS...

ARMOURED CRUISER
SANKT GEORG

ARMOURED CRUISER
KAISER KARL VI

IN JULY 1917 A SMALL DEMONSTRATION AGAINST AUTHORITY WAS QUICKLY SUPPRESSED IN THE AUSTRO-HUNGARIAN NAVY, BUT IN OCTOBER THE CREW OF TORPEDO BOAT II (LEFT) OVERPOWERED THEIR TWO OFFICERS AND SAILED TO ACONA, ITALY. ON 1 FEBRUARY, 1918 A FULL-SCALE MUTINY BROKE OUT IN UNITS OF THE FLEET AT CATTORO AS A RESULT OF WAR-WEARINESS, POOR CONDITIONS, AND COMMUNIST INSPIRATION. THE SAILORS SEIZED THEIR SHIPS, BUT THE THREAT OF TORPEDOING BY LOYAL FLOTILLAS AND THE ARRIVAL OF A DIVISION OF BATTLESHIPS QUICKLY CAUSED THE REVOLT TO COLLAPSE...

25 MAY, 1973: THE GREEK DESTROYER 'VELOS' DROPPED OUT OF A NATO EXERCISE OFF SARDINIA AND SAILED TO THE ITALIAN PORT OF FUMICINO WHERE HER CAPTAIN AND 36 OFFICERS AND MEN OBTAINED POLITICAL ASYLUM AGAINST THE GREEK GOVERNMENT. THE REMAINDER OF THE CREW, UNDER A NEW CAPTAIN, REJOINED THE ALLIED MANOEUVERS WITH THEIR SHIP LATER IN THE MONTH....

MILFORD HAVEN, 1919: EXTREME DIS-CONTENT IN THE ROYAL NAVY OVER THE PAYMENT OF WAR GRATUITIES RESULTED IN THE PATROL BOAT HMS 'KILBRIDE' ACTUALLY HOISTING THE RED FLAG....

5 OCTOBER 1910: THE SAILORS OF THE PORTUGUESE FLEET, LYING IN LISBON HARBOUR, OVERPOWERED AND MURDERED THEIR OFFICERS IN SUPPORT OF A REPUBLICAN REVOLUTION WHICH CAUSED THE KING TO FLEE. THE MUTINOUS SHIPS BOMBARDED THE CITY, DAMAGING THE ROYAL PALACE AND CAUSING MANY CASUALTIES IN THE CIVILIAN POPULACE...

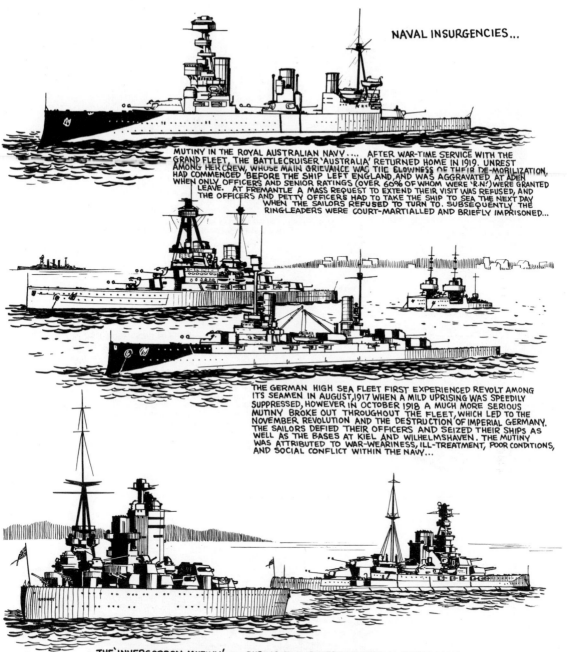

NAVAL INSURGENCIES...

MUTINY IN THE ROYAL AUSTRALIAN NAVY .... AFTER WAR-TIME SERVICE WITH THE GRAND FLEET, THE BATTLECRUISER 'AUSTRALIA' RETURNED HOME IN 1919. UNREST AMONG HER CREW, WHOSE MAIN GRIEVANCE WAS THE SLOWNESS OF THEIR DE-MOBILIZATION, HAD COMMENCED BEFORE THE SHIP LEFT ENGLAND, AND WAS AGGRAVATED AT ADEN WHEN ONLY OFFICERS AND SENIOR RATINGS (OVER 60% OF WHOM WERE 'R.N.') WERE GRANTED LEAVE.   AT FREMANTLE A MASS REQUEST TO EXTEND THEIR VISIT WAS REFUSED, AND THE OFFICERS AND PETTY OFFICERS HAD TO TAKE THE SHIP TO SEA THE NEXT DAY WHEN THE SAILORS REFUSED TO TURN TO. SUBSEQUENTLY THE RINGLEADERS WERE COURT-MARTIALLED AND BRIEFLY IMPRISONED...

THE GERMAN HIGH SEA FLEET FIRST EXPERIENCED REVOLT AMONG ITS SEAMEN IN AUGUST, 1917 WHEN A MILD UPRISING WAS SPEEDILY SUPPRESSED, HOWEVER IN OCTOBER 1918 A MUCH MORE SERIOUS MUTINY BROKE OUT THROUGHOUT THE FLEET, WHICH LED TO THE NOVEMBER REVOLUTION AND THE DESTRUCTION OF IMPERIAL GERMANY. THE SAILORS DEFIED THEIR OFFICERS AND SEIZED THEIR SHIPS AS WELL AS THE BASES AT KIEL AND WILHELMSHAVEN. THE MUTINY WAS ATTRIBUTED TO WAR-WEARINESS, ILL-TREATMENT, POOR CONDITIONS, AND SOCIAL CONFLICT WITHIN THE NAVY...

THE 'INVERGORDON MUTINY' --- DURING THE SEVERE FINANCIAL CRISIS IN 1931 THE BRITISH GOVERNMENT ANNOUNCED DRASTIC CUTS IN NAVAL PAY WITHOUT WARNING OR PROPER EXPLAINATION. SAILORS IN SEVERAL SHIPS OF THE ATLANTIC FLEET (THEN AT INVERGORDON) REFUSED DUTY AND THEIR ACTION BECAME KNOWN AS THE 'INVERGORDON MUTINY'. SUBSEQUENT ENQUIRIES REVEALED THE VERY REAL HARDSHIPS THAT THE REDUCTIONS WOULD IMPOSE, AND THE CUT-BACKS WERE MODIFIED....

NAVAL INSURRECTIONS...

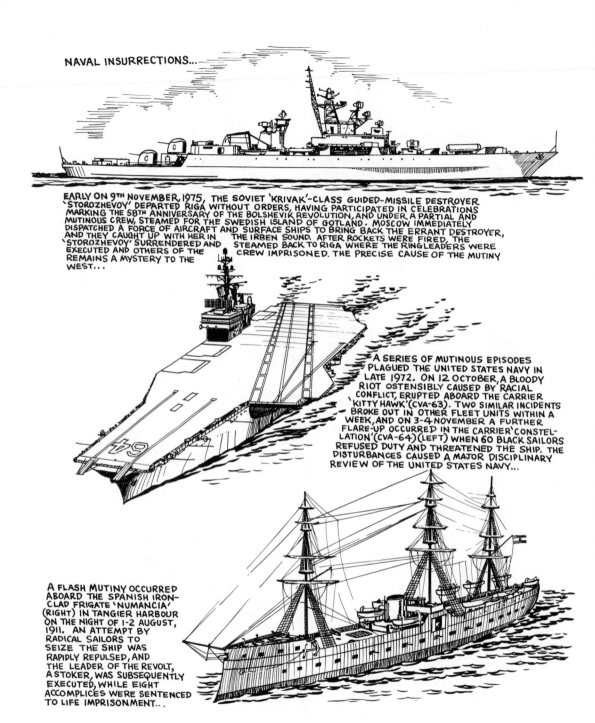

EARLY ON 9TH NOVEMBER, 1975, THE SOVIET 'KRIVAK'-CLASS GUIDED-MISSILE DESTROYER 'STORDZHEVOY' DEPARTED RIGA WITHOUT ORDERS, HAVING PARTICIPATED IN CELEBRATIONS MARKING THE 58TH ANNIVERSARY OF THE BOLSHEVIK REVOLUTION, AND UNDER A PARTIAL AND MUTINOUS CREW, STEAMED FOR THE SWEDISH ISLAND OF GOTLAND. MOSCOW IMMEDIATELY DISPATCHED A FORCE OF AIRCRAFT AND SURFACE SHIPS TO BRING BACK THE ERRANT DESTROYER, AND THEY CAUGHT UP WITH HER IN THE IRBEN SOUND. AFTER ROCKETS WERE FIRED, THE 'STORDZHEVOY' SURRENDERED AND STEAMED BACK TO RIGA WHERE THE RINGLEADERS WERE EXECUTED AND OTHERS OF THE CREW IMPRISONED. THE PRECISE CAUSE OF THE MUTINY REMAINS A MYSTERY TO THE WEST...

A SERIES OF MUTINOUS EPISODES PLAGUED THE UNITED STATES NAVY IN LATE 1972. ON 12 OCTOBER, A BLOODY RIOT OSTENSIBLY CAUSED BY RACIAL CONFLICT, ERUPTED ABOARD THE CARRIER 'KITTY HAWK' (CVA-63). TWO SIMILAR INCIDENTS BROKE OUT IN OTHER FLEET UNITS WITHIN A WEEK, AND ON 3-4 NOVEMBER A FURTHER FLARE-UP OCCURRED IN THE CARRIER 'CONSTELLATION' (CVA-64) (LEFT) WHEN 60 BLACK SAILORS REFUSED DUTY AND THREATENED THE SHIP. THE DISTURBANCES CAUSED A MAJOR DISCIPLINARY REVIEW OF THE UNITED STATES NAVY...

A FLASH MUTINY OCCURRED ABOARD THE SPANISH IRON-CLAD FRIGATE 'NUMANCIA' (RIGHT) IN TANGIER HARBOUR ON THE NIGHT OF 1-2 AUGUST, 1911. AN ATTEMPT BY RADICAL SAILORS TO SEIZE THE SHIP WAS RAPIDLY REPULSED, AND THE LEADER OF THE REVOLT, A STOKER, WAS SUBSEQUENTLY EXECUTED, WHILE EIGHT ACCOMPLICES WERE SENTENCED TO LIFE IMPRISONMENT...

TARGET SHIPS

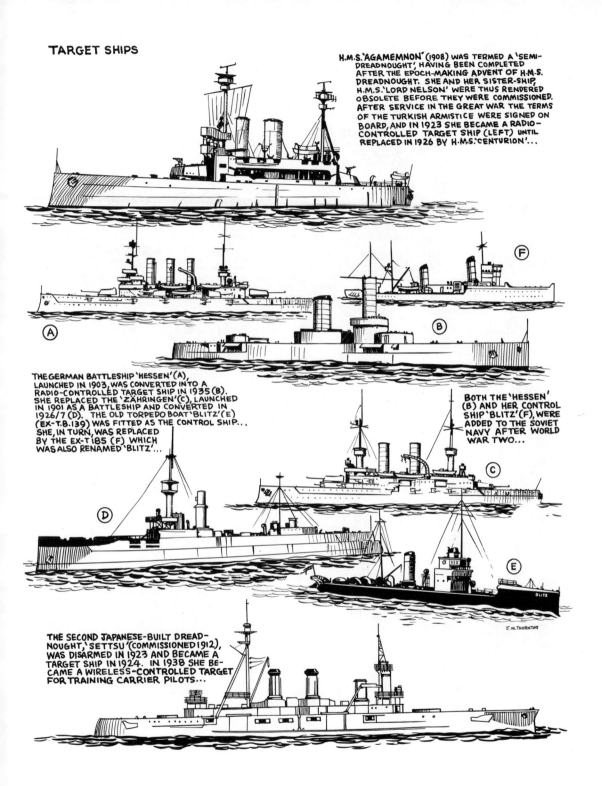

H.M.S. 'AGAMEMNON' (1908) WAS TERMED A 'SEMI-DREADNOUGHT', HAVING BEEN COMPLETED AFTER THE EPOCH-MAKING ADVENT OF H.M.S. DREADNOUGHT. SHE AND HER SISTER-SHIP, H.M.S. 'LORD NELSON' WERE THUS RENDERED OBSOLETE BEFORE THEY WERE COMMISSIONED. AFTER SERVICE IN THE GREAT WAR THE TERMS OF THE TURKISH ARMISTICE WERE SIGNED ON BOARD, AND IN 1923 SHE BECAME A RADIO-CONTROLLED TARGET SHIP (LEFT) UNTIL REPLACED IN 1926 BY H.M.S. 'CENTURION'...

THE GERMAN BATTLESHIP 'HESSEN' (A), LAUNCHED IN 1903, WAS CONVERTED INTO A RADIO-CONTROLLED TARGET SHIP IN 1935 (B). SHE REPLACED THE 'ZÄHRINGEN' (C), LAUNCHED IN 1901 AS A BATTLESHIP AND CONVERTED IN 1926/7 (D). THE OLD TORPEDO BOAT 'BLITZ' (E) (EX-T.B. 139) WAS FITTED AS THE CONTROL SHIP... SHE, IN TURN, WAS REPLACED BY THE EX-T 185 (F) WHICH WAS ALSO RENAMED 'BLITZ'...

BOTH THE 'HESSEN' (B) AND HER CONTROL SHIP 'BLITZ' (F), WERE ADDED TO THE SOVIET NAVY AFTER WORLD WAR TWO...

THE SECOND JAPANESE-BUILT DREAD-NOUGHT, 'SETTSU' (COMMISSIONED 1912), WAS DISARMED IN 1923 AND BECAME A TARGET SHIP IN 1924. IN 1938 SHE BE-CAME A WIRELESS-CONTROLLED TARGET FOR TRAINING CARRIER PILOTS...

J.M. THORNTON

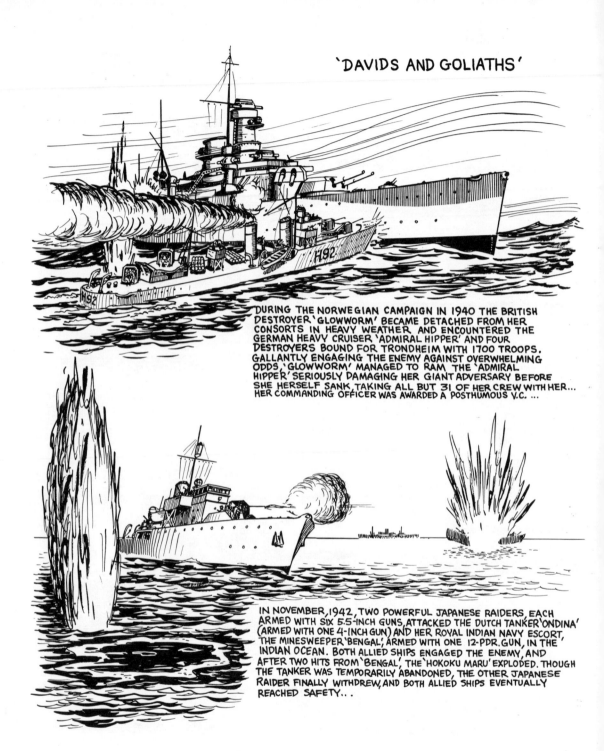

'DAVIDS AND GOLIATHS'

DURING THE NORWEGIAN CAMPAIGN IN 1940 THE BRITISH DESTROYER 'GLOWWORM' BECAME DETACHED FROM HER CONSORTS IN HEAVY WEATHER, AND ENCOUNTERED THE GERMAN HEAVY CRUISER 'ADMIRAL HIPPER' AND FOUR DESTROYERS BOUND FOR TRONDHEIM WITH 1700 TROOPS. GALLANTLY ENGAGING THE ENEMY AGAINST OVERWHELMING ODDS, 'GLOWWORM' MANAGED TO RAM THE 'ADMIRAL HIPPER' SERIOUSLY DAMAGING HER GIANT ADVERSARY BEFORE SHE HERSELF SANK, TAKING ALL BUT 31 OF HER CREW WITH HER... HER COMMANDING OFFICER WAS AWARDED A POSTHUMOUS V.C. ...

IN NOVEMBER, 1942, TWO POWERFUL JAPANESE RAIDERS, EACH ARMED WITH SIX 5.5-INCH GUNS, ATTACKED THE DUTCH TANKER 'ONDINA' (ARMED WITH ONE 4-INCH GUN) AND HER ROYAL INDIAN NAVY ESCORT, THE MINESWEEPER 'BENGAL', ARMED WITH ONE 12-PDR. GUN, IN THE INDIAN OCEAN. BOTH ALLIED SHIPS ENGAGED THE ENEMY, AND AFTER TWO HITS FROM 'BENGAL', THE 'HOKOKU MARU' EXPLODED. THOUGH THE TANKER WAS TEMPORARILY ABANDONED, THE OTHER JAPANESE RAIDER FINALLY WITHDREW, AND BOTH ALLIED SHIPS EVENTUALLY REACHED SAFETY...

ASTONISHING ACTIONS...

ONE OF THE GREATEST SINGLE-SHIP ACTIONS IN HISTORY WAS FOUGHT BETWEEN THE HEAVILY-ARMED GERMAN RAIDER 'STIER' AND THE AMERICAN LIBERTY SHIP 'STEPHEN HOPKINS' IN THE SOUTH ATLANTIC ON 27TH SEPT., 1942. THE RAIDER WAS ARMED WITH SIX 5.9-INCH GUNS, A GUNNERY CONTROL SYSTEM, TWO 37-MM AND FOUR 20-MM GUNS, PLUS TWO TORPEDO TUBES AND TWO SCOUT AIRCRAFT, MANNED BY A TRAINED NAVAL CREW. THE 'STEPHEN HOPKINS' HAD ONE 4-INCH GUN MANNED BY RESERVISTS. WHEN THE GERMAN RAIDER FELL IN WITH THE AMERICAN SHIP, HER CAPTAIN THOUGHT HE WAS UP AGAINST A POWERFUL AUXILIARY CRUISER. AGAINST OVERWHELMING ODDS, THE 'HOPKINS' ENGAGED THE RAIDER, AND SO BADLY CRIPPLED HER THAT SHE WAS ABLAZE BY THE TIME THE GALLANT AMERICAN FOUNDERED. SHORTLY THEREAFTER, THE GERMAN BLEW UP AND FOLLOWED HER ADVERSARY TO THE BOTTOM...

ON 10TH JUNE, 1918, THE TINY (16-TONS) ITALIAN MOTOR LAUNCH 'MAS-15' TORPEDOED THE 22,000-TON 'AUSTRO-HUNGARIAN DREADNOUGHT 'SZENT ISTVÁN' OFF PERMUDA ISLAND NEAR POLA. THE BATTLESHIP ROLLED OVER AND SANK WITH A LOSS OF 90 MEN. LT.CMDR.RIZZO, THE COMMANDER OF THE 'MAS-15' HAD SUNK THE OLD AUSTRO-HUNGARIAN BATTLESHIP 'WIEN' IN A SIMILAR ATTACK AT TRIESTE JUST SIX MONTHS EARLIER!

IN JUNE 1919, DURING THE BALTIC CAMPAIGN, THE 40-FOOT BRITISH COASTAL MOTOR BOAT 'CMB.NO.4' UNDER LT. AUGUSTUS AGAR, ATTACKED THE BOLSHEVIK CRUISER 'OLEG' WHICH WAS BOMBARDING THE FORTRESS OF KRASNAYA GORKA ON KOTLIN ISLAND WHICH WAS HELD BY THE WHITE RUSSIANS. THE TINY CRAFT'S SINGLE TORPEDO STRUCK THE 6650-TON ARMOURED CRUISER, AND WHEN THE RESULTING EXPLOSION WAS OVER THE 'OLEG' HAD DISAPPEARED... LIEUT. AGAR WAS AWARDED THE V.C...

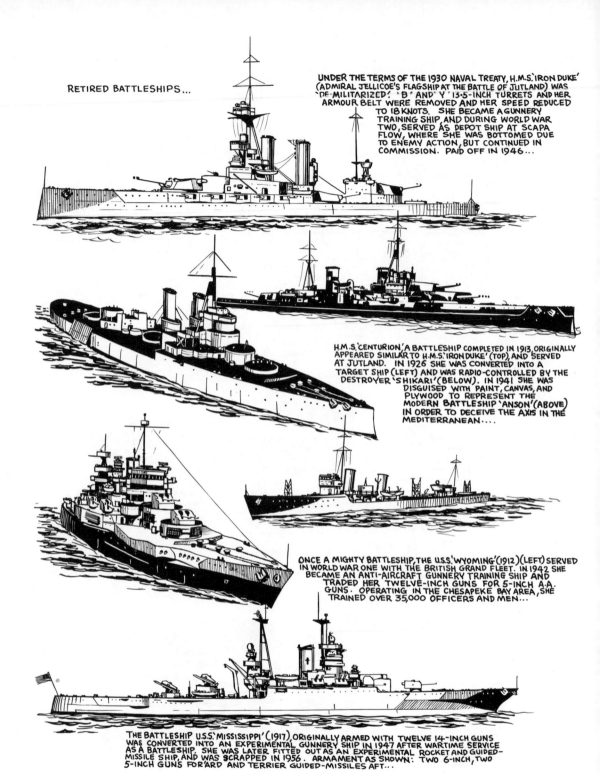

RETIRED BATTLESHIPS...

UNDER THE TERMS OF THE 1930 NAVAL TREATY, H.M.S.'IRON DUKE' (ADMIRAL JELLICOE'S FLAGSHIP AT THE BATTLE OF JUTLAND) WAS 'DE-MILITARIZED'. 'B' AND 'Y' 13·5-INCH TURRETS AND HER ARMOUR BELT WERE REMOVED AND HER SPEED REDUCED TO 18 KNOTS. SHE BECAME A GUNNERY TRAINING SHIP, AND DURING WORLD WAR TWO, SERVED AS DEPOT SHIP AT SCAPA FLOW, WHERE SHE WAS BOTTOMED DUE TO ENEMY ACTION, BUT CONTINUED IN COMMISSION. PAID OFF IN 1946...

H.M.S.'CENTURION', A BATTLESHIP COMPLETED IN 1913, ORIGINALLY APPEARED SIMILAR TO H.M.S.'IRON DUKE' (TOP), AND SERVED AT JUTLAND. IN 1926 SHE WAS CONVERTED INTO A TARGET SHIP (LEFT) AND WAS RADIO-CONTROLLED BY THE DESTROYER 'SHIKARI' (BELOW). IN 1941 SHE WAS DISGUISED WITH PAINT, CANVAS, AND PLYWOOD TO REPRESENT THE MODERN BATTLESHIP 'ANSON' (ABOVE) IN ORDER TO DECEIVE THE AXIS IN THE MEDITERRANEAN....

ONCE A MIGHTY BATTLESHIP, THE U.S.S.'WYOMING'(1912) (LEFT) SERVED IN WORLD WAR ONE WITH THE BRITISH GRAND FLEET. IN 1942 SHE BECAME AN ANTI-AIRCRAFT GUNNERY TRAINING SHIP AND TRADED HER TWELVE-INCH GUNS FOR 5-INCH A.A. GUNS. OPERATING IN THE CHESAPEKE BAY AREA, SHE TRAINED OVER 35,000 OFFICERS AND MEN...

THE BATTLESHIP U.S.S.'MISSISSIPPI'(1917), ORIGINALLY ARMED WITH TWELVE 14-INCH GUNS WAS CONVERTED INTO AN EXPERIMENTAL GUNNERY SHIP IN 1947 AFTER WARTIME SERVICE AS A BATTLESHIP. SHE WAS LATER FITTED OUT AS AN EXPERIMENTAL ROCKET AND GUIDED-MISSILE SHIP, AND WAS SCRAPPED IN 1956. ARMAMENT AS SHOWN: TWO 6-INCH, TWO 5-INCH GUNS FOR'ARD AND TERRIER GUIDED-MISSILES AFT...

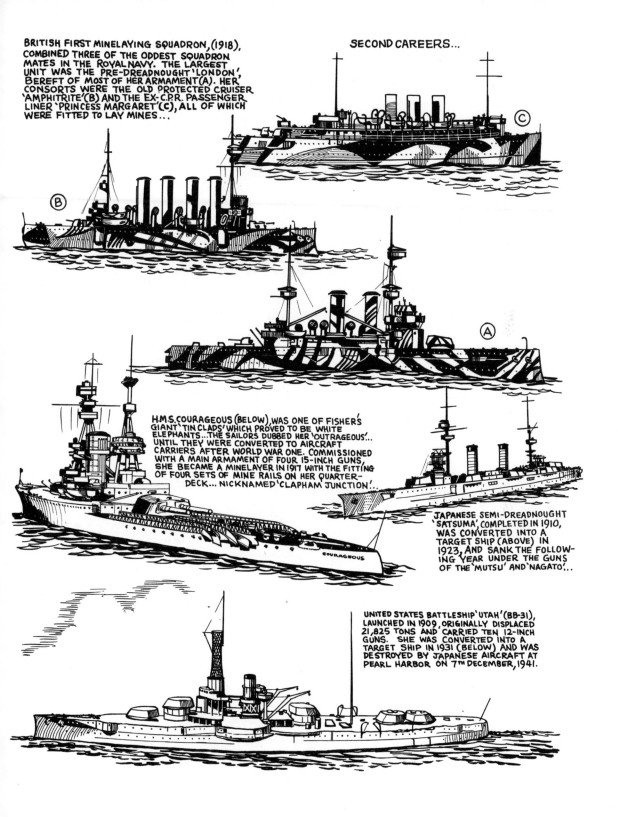

BRITISH FIRST MINELAYING SQUADRON, (1918), COMBINED THREE OF THE ODDEST SQUADRON MATES IN THE ROYAL NAVY. THE LARGEST UNIT WAS THE PRE-DREADNOUGHT 'LONDON', BEREFT OF MOST OF HER ARMAMENT (A). HER CONSORTS WERE THE OLD PROTECTED CRUISER 'AMPHITRITE' (B) AND THE EX-C.P.R. PASSENGER LINER 'PRINCESS MARGARET' (C), ALL OF WHICH WERE FITTED TO LAY MINES...

SECOND CAREERS...

H.M.S. COURAGEOUS (BELOW), WAS ONE OF FISHER'S GIANT 'TIN CLADS' WHICH PROVED TO BE WHITE ELEPHANTS... THE SAILORS DUBBED HER 'OUTRAGEOUS'... UNTIL THEY WERE CONVERTED TO AIRCRAFT CARRIERS AFTER WORLD WAR ONE. COMMISSIONED WITH A MAIN ARMAMENT OF FOUR 15-INCH GUNS, SHE BECAME A MINELAYER IN 1917 WITH THE FITTING OF FOUR SETS OF MINE RAILS ON HER QUARTER-DECK... NICKNAMED 'CLAPHAM JUNCTION'!

JAPANESE SEMI-DREADNOUGHT 'SATSUMA', COMPLETED IN 1910, WAS CONVERTED INTO A TARGET SHIP (ABOVE) IN 1923, AND SANK THE FOLLOWING YEAR UNDER THE GUNS OF THE 'MUTSU' AND 'NAGATO'...

UNITED STATES BATTLESHIP 'UTAH' (BB-31), LAUNCHED IN 1909, ORIGINALLY DISPLACED 21,825 TONS AND CARRIED TEN 12-INCH GUNS. SHE WAS CONVERTED INTO A TARGET SHIP IN 1931 (BELOW) AND WAS DESTROYED BY JAPANESE AIRCRAFT AT PEARL HARBOR ON 7TH DECEMBER, 1941.

FAMOUS FLOTILLAS

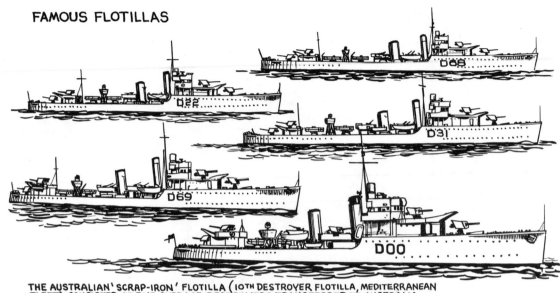

THE AUSTRALIAN 'SCRAP-IRON' FLOTILLA (10TH DESTROYER FLOTILLA, MEDITERRANEAN FLEET), CONSISTED OF FIVE OVER-AGE DESTROYERS TRANSFERRED TO AUSTRALIA FROM GREAT BRITAIN IN 1933... H.M.A. SHIPS 'STUART' (D-00, LEADER), 'VAMPIRE' (D-68), 'WATERHEN' (D-22), 'VENDETTA' (D-69), AND 'VOYAGER' (D-31). CALLED BY THE GERMANS 'THE FIVE OLD PIECES OF SCRAP-IRON THAT AUSTRALIA CALLS HER DESTROYER FLOTILLA', THE OLD VESSELS FOUGHT GALLANTLY. 'WATERHEN' NOW LIES OFF NORTH AFRICA 'VAMPIRE' EAST OF CEYLON, 'VOYAGER' OFF THE TIMOR COAST, WHILE 'VENDETTA' AND 'STUART' 'ESCAPED' TO THE SHIPBREAKERS...

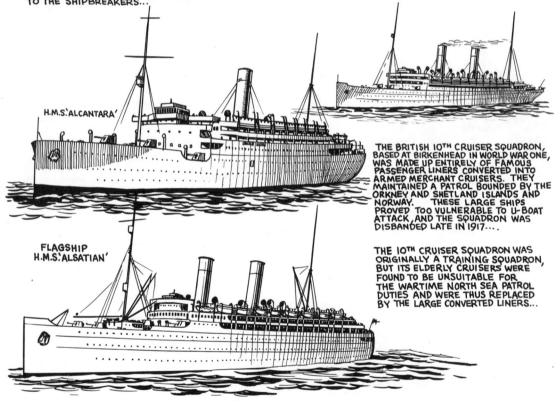

H.M.S. 'ALCANTARA'

FLAGSHIP H.M.S. 'ALSATIAN'

THE BRITISH 10TH CRUISER SQUADRON, BASED AT BIRKENHEAD IN WORLD WAR ONE, WAS MADE UP ENTIRELY OF FAMOUS PASSENGER LINERS CONVERTED INTO ARMED MERCHANT CRUISERS. THEY MAINTAINED A PATROL BOUNDED BY THE ORKNEY AND SHETLAND ISLANDS AND NORWAY. THESE LARGE SHIPS PROVED TOO VULNERABLE TO U-BOAT ATTACK, AND THE SQUADRON WAS DISBANDED LATE IN 1917....

THE 10TH CRUISER SQUADRON WAS ORIGINALLY A TRAINING SQUADRON, BUT ITS ELDERLY CRUISERS WERE FOUND TO BE UNSUITABLE FOR THE WARTIME NORTH SEA PATROL DUTIES AND WERE THUS REPLACED BY THE LARGE CONVERTED LINERS...

WARSHIPS THAT 'CHANGED SIDES'

THE FOUR CHINESE DESTROYERS OF THE 'HAI LUNG' CLASS (BUILT IN GERMANY IN 1898) WERE CAPTURED BY THE BRITISH DESTROYERS 'FAME' AND 'WHITING' AT TAKU IN 1900 DURING THE BOXER UPRISING. THEY WERE THEN DISTRIBUTED TO THE 4 EUROPEAN NAVIES TAKING PART IN THE INTERVENTION, GREAT BRITAIN, GERMANY, FRANCE AND RUSSIA. THE BRITISH AND GERMAN VESSELS WERE BOTH RENAMED 'TAKU', THE FRENCH SHIP BECAME 'TAKOU', WHILE THE RUSSIAN PRIZE BECAME THE 'LT. BOURAKOFF'..

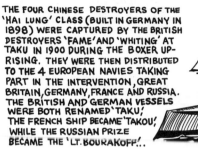

THE TURKISH LIGHT CRUISER 'MEDJIDIEH' (1903), STRUCK A MINE DURING A SORTIE INTO THE BLACK SEA IN APRIL, 1916, AND WAS SUNK BY A CONSORT TO PREVENT HER CAPTURE BY THE RUSSIANS. THIS PROVED TO NO AVAIL, AS THE RUSSIANS QUICKLY SALVED AND REPAIRED HER, AND RENAMED HER 'PRUT.' TWO YEARS LATER, SHE WAS RECAPTURED BY THE TURKS....

A LARGE NUMBER OF RUSSIAN WARSHIPS FELL INTO JAPANESE HANDS AS A RESULT OF THE RUSSO-JAPANESE WAR, AND WERE COMMISSIONED INTO THE IMPERIAL JAPANESE NAVY. THE RUSSIAN 'RETVIZAN' (LEFT), WAS BUILT IN THE U.S.A. AND COMPLETED IN 1902. AFTER SEVERE DAMAGE, SHE WAS SUNK AT PORT ARTHUR, BUT RAISED BY THE JAPANESE IN 1905 AFTER THE FALL OF THE PORT AND COMMISSIONED H.I.J.M.S. 'HIZEN.' THE 'GENERAL ADMIRAL GRAF APRASKIN' (RIGHT) WAS CAPTURED AT THE BATTLE OF TSUSHIMA IN 1905 AND BECAME THE JAPANESE 'OKINOSHIMA'...

WHEN THE ITALIANS INVADED YUGOSLAVIA IN 1941, THEY CAPTURED THE FRENCH-BUILT DESTROYER 'BEOGRAD' AT CATTARO AND RENAMED IT 'SEBENICO' (LEFT). IN 1943, AFTER THE ITALIAN ARMISTICE, IT WAS SEIZED AGAIN, BY THE GERMANS, WHO DESIGNATED IT 'TA43.' THE GERMANS SCUTTLED HER AT TRIESTE IN 1945....

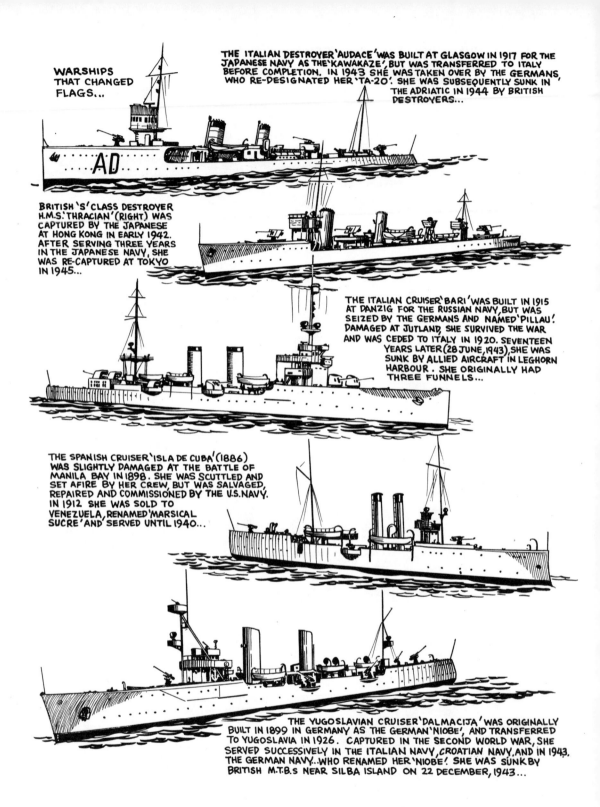

WARSHIPS THAT CHANGED FLAGS...

THE ITALIAN DESTROYER 'AUDACE' WAS BUILT AT GLASGOW IN 1917 FOR THE JAPANESE NAVY AS THE 'KAWAKAZE', BUT WAS TRANSFERRED TO ITALY BEFORE COMPLETION. IN 1943 SHE WAS TAKEN OVER BY THE GERMANS, WHO RE-DESIGNATED HER 'TA-20'. SHE WAS SUBSEQUENTLY SUNK IN THE ADRIATIC IN 1944 BY BRITISH DESTROYERS...

BRITISH 'S' CLASS DESTROYER H.M.S. 'THRACIAN' (RIGHT) WAS CAPTURED BY THE JAPANESE AT HONG KONG IN EARLY 1942. AFTER SERVING THREE YEARS IN THE JAPANESE NAVY, SHE WAS RE-CAPTURED AT TOKYO IN 1945...

THE ITALIAN CRUISER 'BARI' WAS BUILT IN 1915 AT DANZIG FOR THE RUSSIAN NAVY, BUT WAS SEIZED BY THE GERMANS AND NAMED 'PILLAU'. DAMAGED AT JUTLAND, SHE SURVIVED THE WAR AND WAS CEDED TO ITALY IN 1920. SEVENTEEN YEARS LATER (28 JUNE, 1943), SHE WAS SUNK BY ALLIED AIRCRAFT IN LEGHORN HARBOUR. SHE ORIGINALLY HAD THREE FUNNELS...

THE SPANISH CRUISER 'ISLA DE CUBA' (1886) WAS SLIGHTLY DAMAGED AT THE BATTLE OF MANILA BAY IN 1898. SHE WAS SCUTTLED AND SET AFIRE BY HER CREW, BUT WAS SALVAGED, REPAIRED AND COMMISSIONED BY THE U.S. NAVY. IN 1912 SHE WAS SOLD TO VENEZUELA, RENAMED 'MARSICAL SUCRE' AND SERVED UNTIL 1940...

THE YUGOSLAVIAN CRUISER 'DALMACIJA' WAS ORIGINALLY BUILT IN 1899 IN GERMANY AS THE GERMAN 'NIOBE', AND TRANSFERRED TO YUGOSLAVIA IN 1926. CAPTURED IN THE SECOND WORLD WAR, SHE SERVED SUCCESSIVELY IN THE ITALIAN NAVY, CROATIAN NAVY, AND IN 1943, THE GERMAN NAVY...WHO RENAMED HER 'NIOBE'. SHE WAS SUNK BY BRITISH M.T.B.s NEAR SILBA ISLAND ON 22 DECEMBER, 1943...

NAVAL SWITCHES...

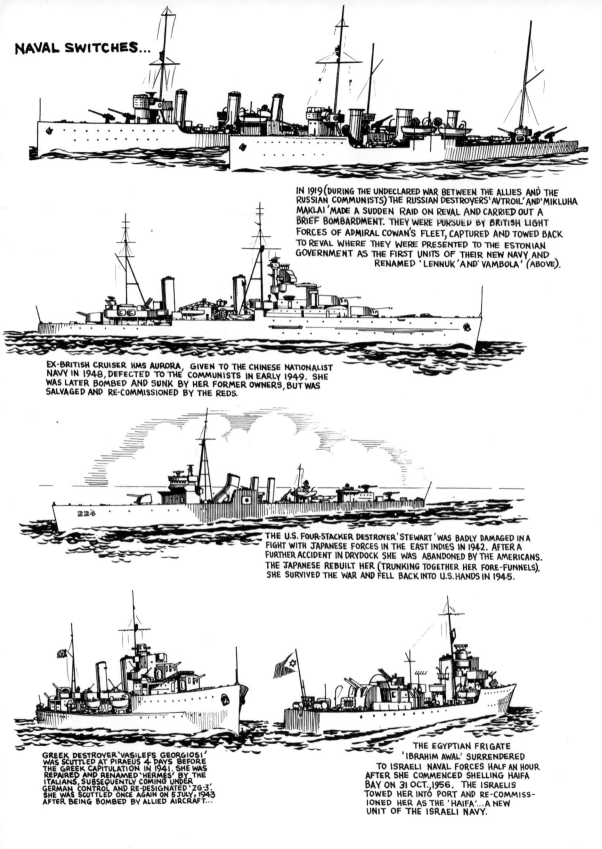

IN 1919 (DURING THE UNDECLARED WAR BETWEEN THE ALLIES AND THE RUSSIAN COMMUNISTS) THE RUSSIAN DESTROYERS 'AVTROIL' AND 'MIKLUHA MAKLAI' MADE A SUDDEN RAID ON REVAL AND CARRIED OUT A BRIEF BOMBARDMENT. THEY WERE PURSUED BY BRITISH LIGHT FORCES OF ADMIRAL COWAN'S FLEET, CAPTURED AND TOWED BACK TO REVAL WHERE THEY WERE PRESENTED TO THE ESTONIAN GOVERNMENT AS THE FIRST UNITS OF THEIR NEW NAVY AND RENAMED 'LENNUK' AND 'VAMBOLA' (ABOVE).

EX-BRITISH CRUISER HMS AURORA, GIVEN TO THE CHINESE NATIONALIST NAVY IN 1948, DEFECTED TO THE COMMUNISTS IN EARLY 1949. SHE WAS LATER BOMBED AND SUNK BY HER FORMER OWNERS, BUT WAS SALVAGED AND RE-COMMISSIONED BY THE REDS.

THE U.S. FOUR-STACKER DESTROYER 'STEWART' WAS BADLY DAMAGED IN A FIGHT WITH JAPANESE FORCES IN THE EAST INDIES IN 1942. AFTER A FURTHER ACCIDENT IN DRYDOCK SHE WAS ABANDONED BY THE AMERICANS. THE JAPANESE REBUILT HER (TRUNKING TOGETHER HER FORE-FUNNELS). SHE SURVIVED THE WAR AND FELL BACK INTO U.S. HANDS IN 1945.

GREEK DESTROYER 'VASILEFS GEORGIOS I' WAS SCUTTLED AT PIRAEUS 4 DAYS BEFORE THE GREEK CAPITULATION IN 1941. SHE WAS REPAIRED AND RENAMED 'HERMES' BY THE ITALIANS, SUBSEQUENTLY COMING UNDER GERMAN CONTROL AND RE-DESIGNATED 'ZG-3'. SHE WAS SCUTTLED ONCE AGAIN ON 5 JULY, 1943 AFTER BEING BOMBED BY ALLIED AIRCRAFT...

THE EGYPTIAN FRIGATE 'IBRAHIM AWAL' SURRENDERED TO ISRAELI NAVAL FORCES HALF AN HOUR AFTER SHE COMMENCED SHELLING HAIFA BAY ON 31 OCT.,1956. THE ISRAELIS TOWED HER INTO PORT AND RE-COMMISSIONED HER AS THE 'HAIFA'... A NEW UNIT OF THE ISRAELI NAVY.

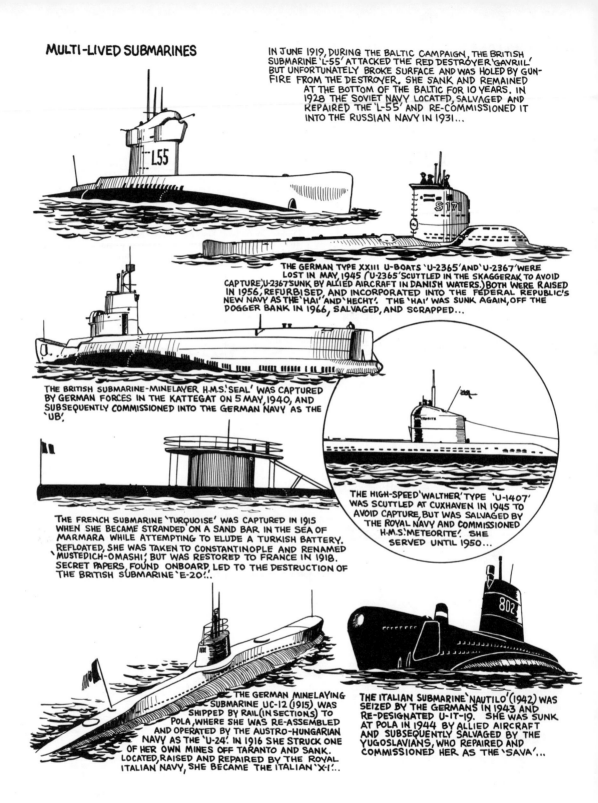

MULTI-LIVED SUBMARINES

IN JUNE 1919, DURING THE BALTIC CAMPAIGN, THE BRITISH SUBMARINE 'L-55' ATTACKED THE RED DESTROYER 'GAVRIIL' BUT UNFORTUNATELY BROKE SURFACE AND WAS HOLED BY GUNFIRE FROM THE DESTROYER. SHE SANK AND REMAINED AT THE BOTTOM OF THE BALTIC FOR 10 YEARS. IN 1928 THE SOVIET NAVY LOCATED, SALVAGED AND REPAIRED THE 'L-55' AND RE-COMMISSIONED IT INTO THE RUSSIAN NAVY IN 1931...

THE GERMAN TYPE XXIII U-BOATS 'U-2365' AND 'U-2367' WERE LOST IN MAY, 1945 ('U-2365' SCUTTLED IN THE SKAGGERAK TO AVOID CAPTURE, 'U-2367' SUNK BY ALLIED AIRCRAFT IN DANISH WATERS.) BOTH WERE RAISED IN 1956, REFURBISED, AND INCORPORATED INTO THE FEDERAL REPUBLIC'S NEW NAVY AS THE 'HAI' AND 'HECHT'. THE 'HAI' WAS SUNK AGAIN, OFF THE DOGGER BANK IN 1966, SALVAGED, AND SCRAPPED...

THE BRITISH SUBMARINE-MINELAYER H.M.S. 'SEAL' WAS CAPTURED BY GERMAN FORCES IN THE KATTEGAT ON 5 MAY, 1940, AND SUBSEQUENTLY COMMISSIONED INTO THE GERMAN NAVY AS THE 'UB'.

THE HIGH-SPEED 'WALTHER' TYPE 'U-1407' WAS SCUTTLED AT CUXHAVEN IN 1945 TO AVOID CAPTURE, BUT WAS SALVAGED BY THE ROYAL NAVY AND COMMISSIONED H.M.S. 'METEORITE'. SHE SERVED UNTIL 1950...

THE FRENCH SUBMARINE 'TURQUOISE' WAS CAPTURED IN 1915 WHEN SHE BECAME STRANDED ON A SAND BAR IN THE SEA OF MARMARA WHILE ATTEMPTING TO ELUDE A TURKISH BATTERY. REFLOATED, SHE WAS TAKEN TO CONSTANTINOPLE AND RENAMED 'MUSTEDICH-OMASHI', BUT WAS RESTORED TO FRANCE IN 1918. SECRET PAPERS, FOUND ONBOARD, LED TO THE DESTRUCTION OF THE BRITISH SUBMARINE 'E-20'...

THE GERMAN MINELAYING SUBMARINE UC-12 (1915) WAS SHIPPED BY RAIL (IN SECTIONS) TO POLA, WHERE SHE WAS RE-ASSEMBLED AND OPERATED BY THE AUSTRO-HUNGARIAN NAVY AS THE 'U-24'. IN 1916 SHE STRUCK ONE OF HER OWN MINES OFF TARANTO AND SANK. LOCATED, RAISED AND REPAIRED BY THE ROYAL ITALIAN NAVY, SHE BECAME THE ITALIAN 'X-1'...

THE ITALIAN SUBMARINE 'NAUTILO' (1942) WAS SEIZED BY THE GERMANS IN 1943 AND RE-DESIGNATED U-IT-19. SHE WAS SUNK AT POLA IN 1944 BY ALLIED AIRCRAFT AND SUBSEQUENTLY SALVAGED BY THE YUGOSLAVIANS, WHO REPAIRED AND COMMISSIONED HER AS THE 'SAVA'...

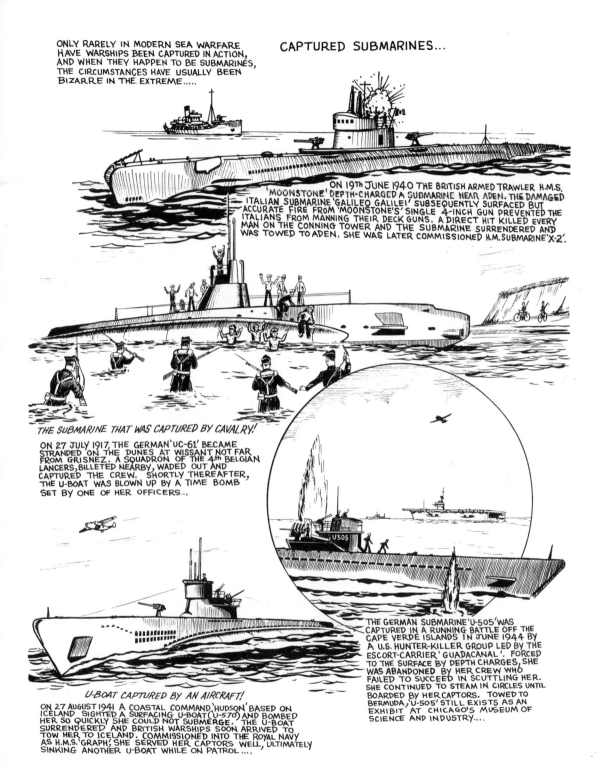

CAPTURED SUBMARINES...

ONLY RARELY IN MODERN SEA WARFARE HAVE WARSHIPS BEEN CAPTURED IN ACTION, AND WHEN THEY HAPPEN TO BE SUBMARINES, THE CIRCUMSTANCES HAVE USUALLY BEEN BIZARRE IN THE EXTREME.....

ON 19th JUNE 1940 THE BRITISH ARMED TRAWLER H.M.S. 'MOONSTONE' DEPTH-CHARGED A SUBMARINE NEAR ADEN. THE DAMAGED ITALIAN SUBMARINE 'GALILEO GALILEI' SUBSEQUENTLY SURFACED BUT ACCURATE FIRE FROM 'MOONSTONE'S' SINGLE 4-INCH GUN PREVENTED THE ITALIANS FROM MANNING THEIR DECK GUNS. A DIRECT HIT KILLED EVERY MAN ON THE CONNING TOWER AND THE SUBMARINE SURRENDERED AND WAS TOWED TO ADEN. SHE WAS LATER COMMISSIONED H.M. SUBMARINE 'X-2'.

THE SUBMARINE THAT WAS CAPTURED BY CAVALRY!

ON 27 JULY 1917, THE GERMAN 'UC-61' BECAME STRANDED ON THE DUNES AT WISSANT NOT FAR FROM GRISNEZ. A SQUADRON OF THE 4th BELGIAN LANCERS, BILLETED NEARBY, WADED OUT AND CAPTURED THE CREW. SHORTLY THEREAFTER, THE U-BOAT WAS BLOWN UP BY A TIME BOMB SET BY ONE OF HER OFFICERS...

U-BOAT CAPTURED BY AN AIRCRAFT!

ON 27 AUGUST 1941 A COASTAL COMMAND 'HUDSON' BASED ON ICELAND SIGHTED A SURFACING U-BOAT ('U-570') AND BOMBED HER SO QUICKLY SHE COULD NOT SUBMERGE. THE U-BOAT SURRENDERED AND BRITISH WARSHIPS SOON ARRIVED TO TOW HER TO ICELAND. COMMISSIONED INTO THE ROYAL NAVY AS H.M.S. 'GRAPH', SHE SERVED HER CAPTORS WELL, ULTIMATELY SINKING ANOTHER U-BOAT WHILE ON PATROL....

THE GERMAN SUBMARINE 'U-505' WAS CAPTURED IN A RUNNING BATTLE OFF THE CAPE VERDE ISLANDS IN JUNE 1944 BY A U.S. HUNTER-KILLER GROUP LED BY THE ESCORT-CARRIER 'GUADACANAL'. FORCED TO THE SURFACE BY DEPTH CHARGES, SHE WAS ABANDONED BY HER CREW WHO FAILED TO SUCCEED IN SCUTTLING HER. SHE CONTINUED TO STEAM IN CIRCLES UNTIL BOARDED BY HER CAPTORS. TOWED TO BERMUDA, 'U-505' STILL EXISTS AS AN EXHIBIT AT CHICAGO'S MUSEUM OF SCIENCE AND INDUSTRY....

EARLY SUBMARINE AIRCRAFT CARRIERS...

U.S. SUBMARINE 'S-1' CARRIED A TINY SEAPLANE WHICH COULD BE ASSEMBLED IN FIVE MINUTES FROM PARTS STORED IN A LARGE STEEL CANISTER ON THE SUBMARINE'S DECK...

THE GIANT FRENCH SUBMARINE 'SURCOUF' (1929) CARRIED A SMALL SEAPLANE IN A SPECIAL HANGAR. SHE WAS DESIGNED FOR OPERATIONS AGAINST TRADE, BUT WAS LOST IN 1942...

BRITISH SUBMARINE 'M-2' (1918) WAS REBUILT IN 1927 TO CARRY A SMALL SCOUT SEAPLANE IN A CYLINDRICAL HANGAR. SHE SANK ACCIDENTALLY IN 1932...

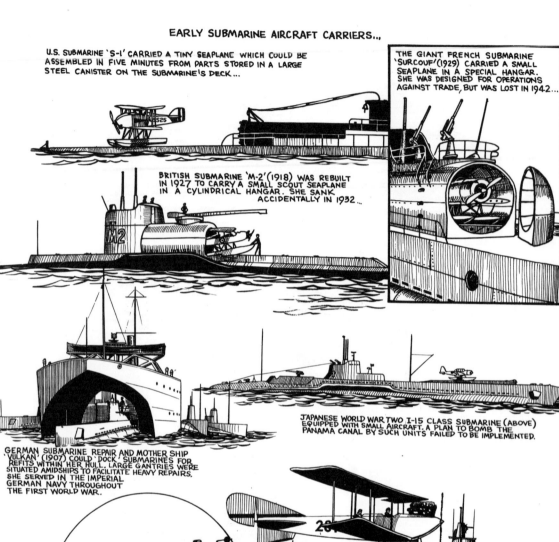

GERMAN SUBMARINE REPAIR AND MOTHER SHIP 'VULKAN' (1907) COULD 'DOCK' SUBMARINES FOR REFITS WITHIN HER HULL. LARGE GANTRIES WERE SITUATED AMIDSHIPS TO FACILITATE HEAVY REPAIRS. SHE SERVED IN THE IMPERIAL GERMAN NAVY THROUGHOUT THE FIRST WORLD WAR.

JAPANESE WORLD WAR TWO I-15 CLASS SUBMARINE (ABOVE) EQUIPPED WITH SMALL AIRCRAFT. A PLAN TO BOMB THE PANAMA CANAL BY SUCH UNITS FAILED TO BE IMPLEMENTED.

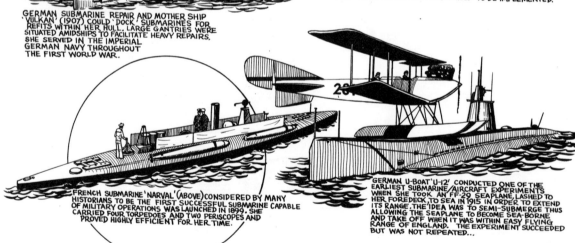

FRENCH SUBMARINE 'NARVAL' (ABOVE) CONSIDERED BY MANY HISTORIANS TO BE THE FIRST SUCCESSFUL SUBMARINE CAPABLE OF MILITARY OPERATIONS WAS LAUNCHED IN 1899. SHE CARRIED FOUR TORPEDOES AND TWO PERISCOPES AND PROVED HIGHLY EFFICIENT FOR HER TIME.

GERMAN U-BOAT 'U-12' CONDUCTED ONE OF THE EARLIEST SUBMARINE AIRCRAFT EXPERIMENTS WHEN SHE TOOK AN FF-29 SEAPLANE, LASHED TO HER FOREDECK, TO SEA IN 1915 IN ORDER TO EXTEND ITS RANGE. THE IDEA WAS TO SEMI-SUBMERGE THUS ALLOWING THE SEAPLANE TO BECOME SEA-BORNE AND TAKE OFF WHEN IT WAS WITHIN EASY FLYING RANGE OF ENGLAND. THE EXPERIMENT SUCCEEDED BUT WAS NOT REPEATED...

EARLY LANDING SHIPS..

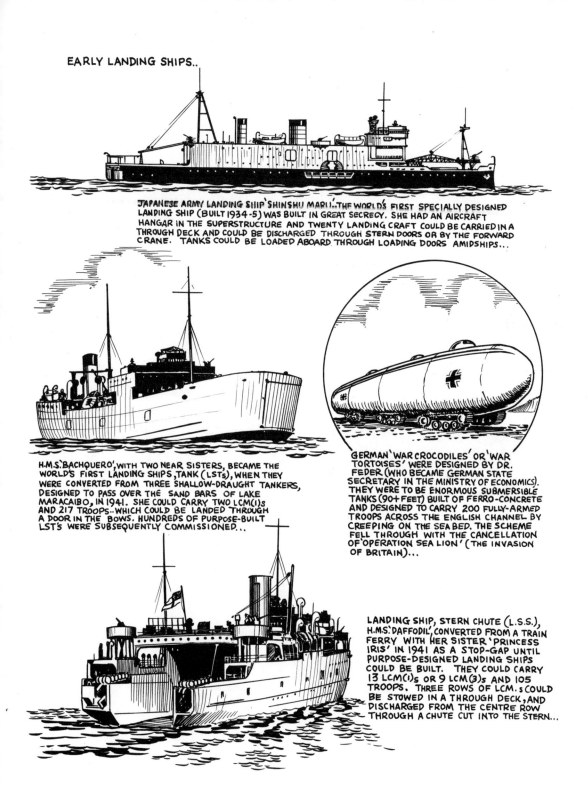

JAPANESE ARMY LANDING SHIP 'SHINSHU MARU'..THE WORLD'S FIRST SPECIALLY DESIGNED
LANDING SHIP (BUILT 1934-5) WAS BUILT IN GREAT SECRECY. SHE HAD AN AIRCRAFT
HANGAR IN THE SUPERSTRUCTURE AND TWENTY LANDING CRAFT COULD BE CARRIED IN A
THROUGH DECK AND COULD BE DISCHARGED THROUGH STERN DOORS OR BY THE FORWARD
CRANE. TANKS COULD BE LOADED ABOARD THROUGH LOADING DOORS AMIDSHIPS...

H.M.S.'BACHQUERO', WITH TWO NEAR SISTERS, BECAME THE
WORLD'S FIRST LANDING SHIPS, TANK (LSTs), WHEN THEY
WERE CONVERTED FROM THREE SHALLOW-DRAUGHT TANKERS,
DESIGNED TO PASS OVER THE SAND BARS OF LAKE
MARACAIBO, IN 1941. SHE COULD CARRY TWO LCM(1)s
AND 217 TROOPS..WHICH COULD BE LANDED THROUGH
A DOOR IN THE BOWS. HUNDREDS OF PURPOSE-BUILT
LST's WERE SUBSEQUENTLY COMMISSIONED...

GERMAN 'WAR CROCODILES' OR 'WAR
TORTOISES' WERE DESIGNED BY DR.
FEDER (WHO BECAME GERMAN STATE
SECRETARY IN THE MINISTRY OF ECONOMICS).
THEY WERE TO BE ENORMOUS SUBMERSIBLE
TANKS (90+ FEET) BUILT OF FERRO-CONCRETE
AND DESIGNED TO CARRY 200 FULLY-ARMED
TROOPS ACROSS THE ENGLISH CHANNEL BY
CREEPING ON THE SEA BED. THE SCHEME
FELL THROUGH WITH THE CANCELLATION
OF 'OPERATION SEA LION' (THE INVASION
OF BRITAIN)...

LANDING SHIP, STERN CHUTE (L.S.S.),
H.M.S.'DAFFODIL', CONVERTED FROM A TRAIN
FERRY WITH HER SISTER 'PRINCESS
IRIS' IN 1941 AS A STOP-GAP UNTIL
PURPOSE-DESIGNED LANDING SHIPS
COULD BE BUILT. THEY COULD CARRY
13 LCM(1)s OR 9 LCM(3)s AND 105
TROOPS. THREE ROWS OF LCM.s COULD
BE STOWED IN A THROUGH DECK, AND
DISCHARGED FROM THE CENTRE ROW
THROUGH A CHUTE CUT INTO THE STERN...

THE 'BATTLES'

THE 24 SHIPS OF THE ROYAL NAVY'S 'BATTLE' CLASS (1942-43) WERE DESIGNED FOR SERVICE IN THE PACIFIC, BUT ONLY 5 UNITS WERE COMPLETED IN TIME TO SERVE IN THAT THEATRE. THEIR DESIGN INCORPORATED A HEAVY A.A. ARMAMENT AND LARGE RADIUS OF ACTION. 15 FURTHER UNITS WERE CANCELLED.

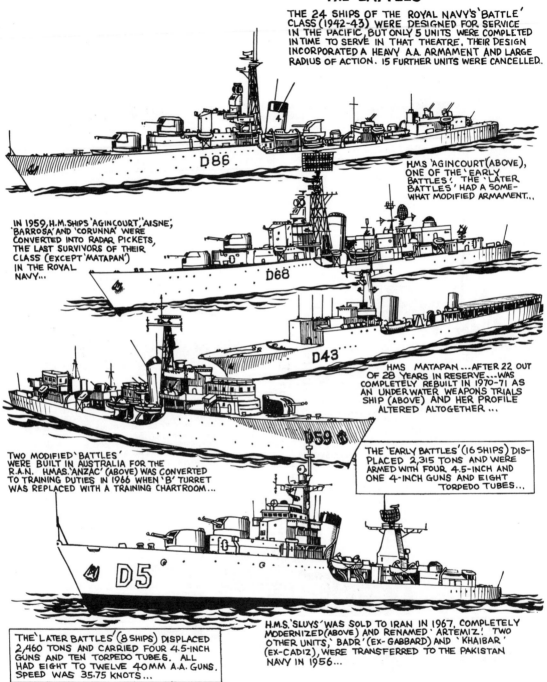

HMS 'AGINCOURT'(ABOVE), ONE OF THE 'EARLY BATTLES'. THE 'LATER BATTLES' HAD A SOME-WHAT MODIFIED ARMAMENT...

IN 1959, H.M.SHIPS 'AGINCOURT', 'AISNE', 'BARROSA' AND 'CORUNNA' WERE CONVERTED INTO RADAR PICKETS, THE LAST SURVIVORS OF THEIR CLASS (EXCEPT 'MATAPAN') IN THE ROYAL NAVY...

HMS MATAPAN ...AFTER 22 OUT OF 28 YEARS IN RESERVE...WAS COMPLETELY REBUILT IN 1970-71 AS AN UNDERWATER WEAPONS TRIALS SHIP (ABOVE) AND HER PROFILE ALTERED ALTOGETHER ...

TWO MODIFIED 'BATTLES' WERE BUILT IN AUSTRALIA FOR THE R.A.N. HMAS.'ANZAC' (ABOVE) WAS CONVERTED TO TRAINING DUTIES IN 1966 WHEN 'B' TURRET WAS REPLACED WITH A TRAINING CHARTROOM...

THE 'EARLY BATTLES' (16 SHIPS) DIS-PLACED 2,315 TONS AND WERE ARMED WITH FOUR 4.5-INCH AND ONE 4-INCH GUNS AND EIGHT TORPEDO TUBES...

THE 'LATER BATTLES' (8 SHIPS) DISPLACED 2,460 TONS AND CARRIED FOUR 4.5-INCH GUNS AND TEN TORPEDO TUBES. ALL HAD EIGHT TO TWELVE 40MM A.A. GUNS. SPEED WAS 35.75 KNOTS...

H.M.S.'SLUYS' WAS SOLD TO IRAN IN 1967, COMPLETELY MODERNIZED(ABOVE) AND RENAMED 'ARTEMIZ'. TWO OTHER UNITS,' BADR' (EX-GABBARD) AND 'KHAIBAR' (EX-CADIZ), WERE TRANSFERRED TO THE PAKISTAN NAVY IN 1956...

GLOSSARY OF TERMS

AA	Anti-aircraft
Accommodation ship	Barracks ship
ASW	Anti-submarine warfare
Aviso	French torpedo gunboat
Barbette	Armoured structure protecting the base of a gun
Breastwork	Armoured parapet
Citadel	Armoured central position containing ship's vitals and armament
C-in-C	Commander-in-Chief
CMB	Coastal Motor Boat
Conning Tower	'Conning' or 'steering' position. Armoured structure in a battleship, also superstructure on a submarine to 'con' the submarine while surfaced
CSS	Confederate States Ship
DE	Destroyer Escort
Dispatch Vessel	Small, fast vessel used to carry dispatches before the general use of wireless
Displacement	Term used to measure the 'weight' of a warship, (i.e.) the weight of the water displaced by the hull
Dreadnought	Revolutionary 12 inch gun battleship (1906) which gave its name to all subsequent battleships as a generic term
En Echelon	Staggered or diagonal
Fairmile	British World War Two motor launch, A/S boat, MTB or MGB named after its designers.
Foc's'le	Forecastle – forward part of a ship, usually occupied by seamen's quarters
Freeboard	The height of a ship's upper deck above the water line

Full Load (FL)	Displacement of a warship fully loaded (i.e. with fuel, ammunition, etc)
HIJMS	His Imperial Majesty's Japanese Ship
HMAS	His (Her) Majesty's Australian Ship
HMCS	His (Her) Majesty's Canadian Ship
HMNS	Her Majesty's Netherlands Ship
HMRAFV	His (Her) Majesty's Royal Air Force Vessel
HMS	His (Her) Majesty's Ship
HQ	Headquarters
Iron Clad	Warship protected with iron or steel plates
Knot	Unit of velocity equal to one nautical mile per hour
LCI	Landing Craft Infantry
LCM	Landing Craft Mechanized
LCT	Landing Craft Tank
LSS	Landing Ship Stern Chute
LST	Landing Ship Tank
ML	Motor Launch
MLR	Muzzle-loading rifled
Monitor	Shallow draught vessel, armed with heavy guns for coastal bombardment
MS	Motor Ship
MTB	Motor Torpedo Boat
P & O	Peninsular & Orient Line
Poop	A short deck above the upper deck right aft
Pre-Dreadnought	Battleship of the period between the 'Line-of-Battleship' era and the advent of HMS *Dreadnought* (1906)
PT	US Navy designation for Motor Torpedo Boat (Patrol Torpedo Boat)
Q-Ship	Disguised warship or merchant ship with concealed weapons used to lure an enemy
Ram Bow	Protruding armoured bow designed to ram an enemy ship
RAN	Royal Australian Navy
RCMP	Royal Canadian Mounted Police
RCN	Royal Canadian Navy
Receiving Ship	Accommodation or barracks ship
Refit	Repair/major maintenance of a ship
RN	Royal Navy
RNVR	Royal Naval Volunteer Reserve
Screw	Propeller

Semi-Dreadnought	Post-Dreadnought with mixed main armament (two calibres)
Sloop	Small cruising gunboat, also used as an escort
Spar Deck	Raised after deck on a rigged ship used to accommodate spars, timbers, spare yards, etc
SSM	Surface to surface missile
Super-Dreadnought	Dreadnought armed with 13·5 inch guns or larger
Superstructure	That portion of a ship built above the hull containing bridgeworks, etc
Tumblehome	The sides of a ship near the upper deck inclining inwards are said to 'tumble home'
Turret	Armoured mounting for the protection of one or more guns
USN	United States Navy
USS	United States Ship
VC	Victoria Cross

INDEX OF SHIPS

Abercrombie 21, 41
Adler 55
Admiral Hipper 85
Agamemnon 87
Agincourt 98
Aisne 98
Akagi 16, 17, 43
Alabama 25, 28, 32
Alaska 45
Alaska 16
Alexandra 8
Alliance 34
Almaz 74
Almirante Brown 53
Almirante Cochrane 26
Almirante Saldhana 79
Alton 26
Amagi 43
Amber 77
America 76
Amethyst 26
Amiral Baudin 9
Amphitrite 69, 89
Andrew 34, 36
Anson 88
Anzac 98
Aquitania 58
Argus 16
Arizona 36
Ark Royal 59, 60
Artemiz 98
Asahi 10
Ashville 49
Atheling 67
Athenia 76
Attacker 67
Audace 92
Aurora 27, 93
Australia 83
Averof 27
Avtroil 93
Awatea 58
Azova 81
B-1 62
Bachni Saltatori 47
Bachquero 97
Balao 32
Balilla 72
Bangor 78
Banning 31
Barham 59
Bari 92
Barnes 67

Barnstaple 68
Barrosa 98
Batfish 32
Bathurst 29
Becuna 32
Belfast 29
Belknap 60
Bengall 85
Beograd 91
Biber 51
Biga 78
Blanco Encalada 26
Blitz 87
Bombe 13
Borodino 42
Bowfin 32
Bremen 56
Brennus 9
Breslau 11
Buck 58
Buffel 26
Bulwark 63
Burza
Bustard 20
Daffodil 97
Dale 69
Dalmacija 92
Defiance 12
Delphin 51
Delphy 56
Derski 29
Devastation 8
Dolphin 31, 36
Drum 28, 32
Duchess 59
Dufferin 79
Duilio 12
Duke of York 56
Dunkerque 19
Dupuy de Lome 72
Cadiz 98
Calcutta 59
Calliope 55
Campania 67
Camperdown 56
Carib Queen 73
Carlo Alberto 71
Caroline 29
Carraciolo 42
Castel Forte 67
Castle 70
Castlemaine 29
Cavalier 30

Cavalla 32
Centurion 88
Cerberus 26, 29
Chariot 47
Charybdis 70
Chemung 58
Chicago 26
Clapham Junction 89
Classic 30
Clemenceau 41
Cleopatra 76
CMB No 4 86
CMB 103 31
Cobia 32
Colossus 8
Condorcet 10
Constellation 23, 84
Constitucion 49
Constitution 23
Corsair 77
Conway 24
Corunna 98
Courageous 16, 21, 89
Crane Ship No 1 70
Cressy 24
Curacoa 59
Curley 21
E-20 94
Eagle 17, 77
Eber 55
Edinburgh 8
Elco 48
Empire Parkeston 66
Ersatz Yorck 43
Espana 57
Essex 31
Europa 15
Fairsky 67
Fame 91
Fearless 61
Fenian Ram 34
Flasher 32
Fletcher 30
Flounder 61
Ford 72
Foresight 14
Formidable 9
Forward 14
Foudre 12, 15
Foudroyant 24
Flower 66
France 57
Francesco Carraciolo 42

Frank E. Evans 60
Fraser 59
Furios 16, 20, 36
Gabbard 98
Gagnut 57
Galileo Galilei 95
Gannet 24
Gavril 94
Gefion 71
General Admiral Graf Apraskin 91
General Botha 79
General Wolfe 71, 20
Glacier Queen 68
Gladiator 58
Glatton 63
Glenmore 18
Gloire 9
Glorious 21, 16
Gloucester 77
Glowworm 85
Gneisenau 19
Goeben 11, 21
Goteborg 62
Graph 95
Guadalcanal 33, 95
Guam 19
Guepe 18
Guilio Cesare 63
Gulf Mariner 78
Gulf Wing 68
Hai 94
Haida 30
Haifa 93
Hai Lung 91
Hambro 73
Hannibal 71
Havelock 21
Hawke 58
Hecht 94
Herchmer 78
Hermes 16, 93
Hessen 87
Higgins 48
Highway 16, 73
Hindustan 81
Hipper 44
Hiryu 17
Hizan 91
Hobson 60
Hoche 9
Hoe 61
Hohenzollern 74, 75
Hokoku Maru 85

Hood 36
Horno 39
Hosho 16
Hotspur 12
Huascar 26
Hudson 95
Humber 69
Hussar 62
I–15 96
Ibrahim Awal 93
Idaho 10
Illinois 25, 38
Imperator Alexander I 15
Imperator Nikolai I 15
Imperatrista Maria 63
Implacable 24
Inaugral 31
Independence 25
Indiana 37
Infanta 77
Inflexible 61
Ingraham 58
Intelligent Whale 34
Iron Duke 63, 88
Isla de Cuba 92
Italia 66
Jamshed Nussernanji 38
Jastrzab 62
J. F. Kennedy 60
Joseph P. Kennedy 32
Joseph P. Kennedy Jr. 30
JU–64, 88
Juneau 30
Jupiter 71
K-4 61
K-6 61
K-11 43
K-14 61
K-17 61
K-21 33
K-22 61
Kaga 16, 17, 43
Kairyu 52
Kaiseradler 75
Kaiten 47
Kawakaze 92
Kearsage 70
Khaibar 98
Kilbride 82
Kilkis 10
King Edward 21
King George V 59
Kitty Hawk 84
Klas Horn 62
Klas Uggla 62
Königin Luise 36
Königsberg 69
Koryu 50
Koylin 60
Krivak 84
Kronstadt 45
L-55 94
Lady Cecilia 68
Lady Cynthia 68

Lance 36
Landfall 73
Landrale 36
Langley 16
Leaside 68
Leberecht Maass 62
Leipzig 59
Lemnos 10
Lennuk Vambola 93
Leonardo da Vinci 63
Letitia 58
Levrier 13
Lexington 17
Lionfish 30, 32
Little Rock 30
London 63, 89
Long Island 67
Lord Clive 20
Lord Nelson 87
LSM 230 73
Lt. Bourakoff 91
Luctor et Emergo 34
Lung Wei 8
Lützow 44
Lyon 41
Lysistrata 76
MacBrien 78
Mackensen 43
Magnificent 71
Maine 11
Mala 52
Marder 47
Margaree 59
Mars 71
Marshal Soult 21
Marsical Sacre 92
Marte 37
Marti 74
MAS-15 31, 86
Masay 69
Massachusetts 28, 30, 32
Matagalpa 69
Matapan 98
Matsushima 63
Max Schultz 62
Medea 77
Medicine Hat 78
Medjidieh 91
Melbourne 60
Melton 68
Memphis 55
Mercury 24
Meteorite 94
Mikasa 27
Mikluha Maklai 93
Minas Geraes 81
Minotaur 44
Mississippi 10, 88
Molch 51
Moonstone 95
Montagu 57
Montebello 13
MTB-234 31
MTB-378 48

Mtsu 89
Musashi 20
Mustedich-Omashi 94
Mutsu 63
Nagato 89
Nanuchka 49
Narval 96
Narwhal 37
Nashville 70
Nautilo 94
New Hampshire 25
Nikolai 1 8
Nile 24
Ning Hai 53
Nino Bixio 14
Niobe 92
Nipsic 55
North Carolina 28
Novorossiysk 63
Numancia 84
Oakham Castle 70
Oaxaca 66
Oceanographer 77
Oka 74
Okinoshima 91
Old Ironsides 23
Oleg 86
Olga 55
Olive Branch 61
Olympia 27
Olympic 58
Ondina 85
Oregon 35
Orien 73
Orizaba 76
Osborne 69
Ostfriesland 36
Outrageous 89
Oxley 62
P-514 62
P-551 62
Pacific Gold 68
Pacific Venture 68
Paek-Ku 49
Panther 11
Parch 32
Parramatta 35
Partenope 13
Papanikolis 35
Penelope 76
Peony 72
Peral 34
Peruvier 72
Petropavlovsk 44
Pillau 92
Ping Hai 53
Pioneer 34
Plongeur 34
Polaris 77
Poltava 44
Pommern 19
Port Fairy 59
Portland 37
Potemkin 81

Prairie State 25
President Garcia 66
Presidente Sarmiento 29
Prince 21
Prince Henry 66
Princess Iris 97
Princess Margaret 89
Prinz Eugen 59
Prut 91
Puglia 35
Punjabi 59
Putnam 69
Queen Mary 59
Queen of Thanet 68
Raglan 21
Raleigh 57
Ramilles 36
Ranger 17
Rattlesnake 13
Recruit 38, 39
Reina Mercedes 25
Renown 75
Reshef 49
Resolution 36
Retvizan 91
Roberts 21
Roma 67
Roncador 32
Rusalka 55
S-1 96
Sailfish 35
Sakuma 34
Salamis 41
Salvage Chief 73
San Francisco 35
Sao Paulo 81
Sapphire 111 76
Saratoga 17
Satsuma 89
Sava 94
Scharnhorst 17, 19, 29, 45, 56
Schlesien 10
Schleswig-Holstein 10
Schorpioen 26
Seaham 78
Seal 94
Sebenico 91
Seeandbee 18
Seehund 51
Settsu 87
Sevastopol 45
Seven Seas 67
Seydlitz 44
Shah 26
Shaw 58
Shikari 88
Shikishima 10
Shinano 20
Shinshu Maru 97
Shinyo 17
Shinyo 47
Shrimp 52
Shtandart 74
Silverstein 62

Skirmisher 14
Sleipner 74
Sluys 98
Smiter 66
Sofia 66
Soryu 17
Southern Cross 76
Sovietsky Soyuz 45
Sovietsky Ukraina 45
Sovietskaya Bielorossiya 45
Spica 49
Sprat 52
Squalus 35
St Paul 58
St Stephen 70
St Thomas 68
Stack 60
Stalingrad 45
Stephen Hopkins 86
Stewart 93
Stickleback 52, 62
Stier 86
Storozhevoy 84
Strana Sovietov 45
Strasbourg 19
Stuart 90
Sudbury 68
Sultan Selim 11
Sunfish 62
Surcouf 39, 96
Swindon 68
SX 404 52
Sydney 35

Szent Istvan 31, 86
T-185 87
TA-20 92
TA-43 91
Tabasco 69
Takou 91
Taku 91
Tallin 44
Tang 64
Teapa 69
Texas 28
Thames 79
The Sullivans 30
Thea Foss 77
Thracian 92
Thunderer 8
Tiger 62
Tirpitz 33, 66
Tonnant 9
Tonnerre 9
Tosa 43
Trailer Princess 73
Trenton 55
Tribal 30
Trinacria 76
Trincomalee 24
Trinidad 64
Triton 62
Trois Revieres 78
Tromp 53
Truro 78
Tullibee 64
Turquoise 94

Type T14 MTB 48
U-1 33
U-12 96
U-24 94
U-28 61
U-439 61
U-459 61
U-505 33, 95
U-570 95
U-659 61
U-955 33
U-1407 94
U-2365 94
U-2367 94
UB 94
UC-5 39
UC-61 95
U-IT-19 94
Umpire 62
Undaunted 15
Unicorn 24
Utah 89
Vampire 90
Vandalia 58
Vanguard 21, 63
Vasilefs Georgiosi 93
Vassilevs Georgis 21, 41
Veintecinco de Maya 53
Velos 82
Vendetta 90
Vessikko 33
Victoria 56
Victory 23

Vindictive 35
Vorovsky 76
Voyager 60, 90
Vulcan 12
Vulkan 96
Walther 94
Ward 36
Warrior 25
Wasp 60
Wateree 55
Waterhen 90
Weather Reporter 70
Wellington 61
West Virginia 37
Whiting 91
Wolverine 18
Worcester 24
Worden 69
Wyoming 88
X-1 94
X-2 95
Yamato 20
Yankton 76
Yavuz 11
Yorktown 31
Yubari 53
Yukon Star 68
Z-26 64
Zähringen 87
Zaragoza 76
ZC-2 93
Zenson 71